"Regina Coll's book, *Christianity and Feminism in Conversation*, is a helpful contribution to the growing literature of Christian feminist theology. Coll places feminist theology within the context of liberation theology and reaches out to the new voices of Third World feminist theologians. At the same time, she brings a wide-ranging exploration of feminist thought into conversation with all the major themes of classical Christian systematic theology in a way that should help make feminist reflection more accessible to those in colleges and seminaries.

"At a time when there is increasing poverty among women and children throughout the world, growing violence against women, and a mounting effort to attack feminism as anti-Christian, Coll makes clear that not only can Christianity come into dialogue with feminism, but that this conversation is essential to the recovery of the gospel today."

Rosemary Radford Ruether
Georgia Harkness Professor of Applied Theology
Garrett-Evangelical Theological Seminary

"If I were to select one book that gives an overview of Christian/Catholic Feminist theology, this would be it. Regina Coll's extremely clear voice, accessible style, and thorough scholarship make it accessible to all: women and men, ordinary readers, undergraduate and graduate students. A primer, a guide, and a summation all between two covers!"

Maria Harris
Author, *Dance of the Spirit:*
*The Seven Steps of Women's Spirituality*

"This text resounds with the voice of a wise teacher who moves easily in the worlds of both her subjects. Regina Coll demonstrates that the contemporary feminist critique of the Christian tradition raises exciting prospects for development as well as demands for deconstruction. Throughout, the reader is invited to participate in the process, shaping Christian feminism through the questions and suggested exercises that accompany each chapter. I know of no better introduction to the overall theological concerns of Christian feminists than this beautifully balanced work."

Mary Aquin O'Neill, RSM, Director
Mount Saint Agnes Theological Center for Women

"Regina Coll notes that 'to enter into conversation with a book is to advance the conversation, challenge some ideas, affirm others, and create new knowledge.' The style of this volume, replete with reflection questions for each chapter, invites the reader into the ongoing conversation between Christianity's foundational elements and feminist insights. While other studies focus on single issues, this significant work invites the reader into the broad sweep of feminist approaches to anthropological, theological, and ethical issues, culminating in a living spirituality. Those who engage in conversation with the author through this book cannot but be enriched."

John Allyn Melloh, S.M.
University of Notre Dame

# CHRISTIANITY
# & FEMINISM
## in
# CONVERSATION

## REGINA A. COLL

TWENTY-THIRD PUBLICATIONS
Mystic, Connecticut 06355

Twenty-Third Publications
185 Willow Street
P.O. Box 180
Mystic, CT 06355
(203) 536-2611
800-321-0411

ISBN 0-89622-579-8
Library of Congress Catalog Card Number 93-79451
Printed in the U.S.A.

# Dedication

For my nieces:
Mary Anne, Joan, Regina, Thea, Eileen,
Tracy, and Kim

# Acknowledgments

My journey into feminism began with Alice Pease Coll, a woman ahead of her time. It has been enriched by the many women who have shared their wisdom and their questions with me during lectures, retreats and courses.

Special thanks go to Carole Coffin, John Melloh and Mark Poorman who make my life and work at Notre Dame a joy.

Thanks also to the Sisters of St. Joseph, my good friends Helen Costello and Joanmarie Smith and my sister/friend Judith, whose words of encouragement mean more than she could ever know.

# Contents

# Introduction

For twenty years I have been lecturing and teaching—in India, Scotland, Canada, as well as the United States—about the role of women in the church. Over the years I have become more and more aware that many women are struggling to bring their feminist ideas and their Christian faith into dialogue. They have expressed a desire for theological insights that might support or challenge feminism and for feminist theory that might support or challenge Christianity. I believe that feminist theologians (both female and male) have already opened the way for this kind of dialogue to happen. They have begun the conversation and are in the process of bringing forth a deeper understanding of both Christianity and feminism. The conversation I propose in this book continues this process. It takes the compatibility of Christianity and feminism so seriously that it may better be called Christian feminism in conversation with itself.

Getting involved in a conversation implies a give and take, a sharing of ideas, a donation of oneself. Cocktail party chatter is not really conversation. Debates and arguments are not conversations; nor is eavesdropping on the conversation of others. Respectful listening to the other and the sincere sharing of one's own insights are key elements in real conversations.

1

While involvement in a conversation demands openness to new ideas, it does not suppose unquestioning acceptance of every idea. Stimulating conversations bring challenging opinions, exciting concepts, and strong convictions to bear on one another. They help participants to sharpen their own ideas and articulate them better. In setting up this particular conversation, I have attempted to be faithful to three basic principles. The first is that we *can* remain loyal to our tradition while responding to the signs of our times. What I do here is to examine ways of transmitting the excellence of the Christian message that overcome the destructive patriarchal and hierarchical character of some interpretations throughout history. I also cite the works of feminist theologians who present fresh insights into the myths, symbols, and beliefs of Christianity and that challenge readers to struggle with difficult issues from an alternative perspective.

The second principle is that both the *rational* study of theology—which is academic, intellectual, and sedimented in creeds and dogmas—and the *experiential*—which is extra-rational, relational, and rooted in the narratives, myths, rituals, and symbols of the faithful—are necessary for a more adequate understanding of Christianity. The development of theology does not happen in a vacuum but in the life and reflection of the community. All theology grows out of the concerns and tensions of a particular age. Professional theologians use the tools of theology to express the truths of Christianity in terms intelligible to their peers (and sometimes to the rest of the Christian community). But so-called amateur theologians also reflect on events in the light of the gospel and tradition and thus contribute to the theological enterprise.

The third principle I tried to follow is to remain alert to the contributions of those people whose voices have not been sufficiently heard: the women of Asia, Africa, Latin America, and the women of the third world imbedded within the first world. I have, in the process, been introduced to some of the most exciting feminist theology being developed, and I have whenever possible tried to incorporate it into my thoughts and writings. In this, of course, I am an outsider.

## The Sequence of Chapters

Chapter 1 sets guidelines and parameters for the conversation. Theology, liberation theology, and feminist liberation theology set the stage for the discussions to follow.

The conversation begins in earnest in Chapter 2 with God who is the Source and Ground of all that is. Images of God and interpretations of doctrines about God affect not only our relationship with God but also the way we view the universe and ourselves. Belief in God sets the context of the whole conversation.

Chapter 3 speaks about Jesus Christ, truly divine and truly human. The teaching, life, death, and resurrection of Jesus reveal what God is like in human form. While Christology is said to be the doctrine that has been used against women more than any other, some feminist theologians are attempting to recover Christology from those negative elements.

Chapter 4 presents alternative perspectives on what it means to be human. A person's image of God and image of self are so closely related that to alter one is to radically alter the other.

History has not always included the experience of women in deliberations about the meaning of life. Introducing those missing pieces is not simply a "mix together and stir" process. Something entirely new is in the process of creation that transforms the image of both male and female human beings.

Mary, true disciple of Christ, is the subject of Chapter 5. Somewhat forgotten in recent times, Mary is being reclaimed as a model for the church and for all Christians, not just women.

I put off the conversation about good and evil until Chapter 6 in the hope that it will be viewed in a different light as a result of the preceding exchanges.

Our foremothers in scripture are the focus of Chapters 7 and 8. New wisdom about God and ourselves provides the means to reclaim our roots. Searching the scriptures furnishes instances that demean women; it also furnishes instances that champion the cause of women. The hope is that we will be able to read the bible with new eyes, perhaps to see what had been hidden before. This will mean denouncing negative principles and announcing the good news that has sometimes been overlooked.

The conversation comes full circle in Chapter 9 with some words about spirituality. Spirituality is the process whereby we live out relationships with God, others, and ourselves. It is the word we have used in the past to describe our "inner life." Here I use it as the word that describes the aim of feminist theology: the enrichment of each individual's and the Christian community's movement toward God.

# $\mathcal{F}$eminist $\mathcal{T}$heologies

$\mathcal{F}$aith seeking understanding—that's how St. Anselm described theology. While not always called theology, this seeking of understanding by human beings appears to be a universal phenomenon. The artifacts of prehistoric times indicate that our ancestors tried to make sense of the mysterious powers at work in their world. Neanderthals buried their dead with food and tools, perhaps as a result of their reflection on the possibility of an afterlife. Their cave drawings illustrate a reverence for the cave bear. While we have no Neanderthal texts we can infer that these people understood in some primitive way that they were not independent of the mysterious forces beyond them. They attempted to relate to and perhaps control those forces.

The litany of written works that are available to us provide ample proof of the penchant for theological reflection through the ages: the Gilgamesh Epic, the works of Homer and Hesiod, dramas of Aeschylus, Sophicles and Euripides, the Upanishads, the Four Books of the disciples of Confucius, to name but a few, are examples of faith seeking understanding.

Theology is an effort to bring our experience of God to some intellectual expression. For the most part and until recently, what we strictly name theology has been developed in monasteries and universities and is the result of logical and rational arguments. Systematically developed, theology has both conserved the past and reinterpreted it for each succeeding generation. Theology searches for clues to the great questions of humanity: What does it mean to be human? Who or what is God? What is humanity's relationship to God? What does it mean to live a good life? Why death? Why does evil exist?...

But simply studying these questions does not constitute theology. Philosophers wrestle with similar questions and their work does not necessarily constitute theology. Theology arises out of a believing community. Theology presupposes religion and religion presupposes faith. It is a third moment that grows out of the other two; it does not give rise to the other two. Without faith there is no religion and without religion there is no theology. Faith is a personal experiential knowledge of God. Religion is the institutionalized, external expression of that faith. And theology is the attempt to understand the symbols, myths, rituals, and metaphors of religion.

Theology is not simply a body of knowledge to be studied, not simply a passing on intact and unchanged the wisdom of another age. While the insights of the past certainly do contribute to the theological enterprise, theology is a process, an action done in the present. In this chapter, I will discuss theology, one of its branches known as liberation theology, and then set feminist theology under the rubric of liberation theology.

### Theology Is Incomplete

Theology is incomplete knowledge. God is not finished acting in this world; the Spirit is still abiding with us, leading us, calling us, urging us to become all we were created to be. Theology is not simply a reflection on God's revelation in the past, in the history of the Hebrews, and the life and teaching of Jesus. It is more an attempt to understand God's revelation today, here and now, as understood in the light of past revelation. Theologians attempt to describe this abiding presence of God by a variety of multivalenced metaphors, symbols, analogies, and methodologies. Theology probes God's involvement with humanity in the past and projects what God's future may look like; but theology ordinarily addresses the issues of each particular age. A quick look at the development of doctrine reveals the connections between the social and political realities of each age and theological development. We who believe that God is not only a God of nature but a God involved in history have ever new insights about which to theologize. We, then, are constantly learning more about the ways of God with humanity.

Theology is incomplete also because human beings can know only in part. The theology of every age is limited by the cultural, political, aesthetic, and scientific insights of that age. For example, Thomas Aquinas' theology about the nature of women suffers because of the primitive science available to him. Believing that all life was contained in the male seed and that a seed should produce according to its own kind, Thomas perceived women as "defective and misbegotten males," a conclusion he could not make in light of today's scientific knowledge. History also reveals theological justification for the divine right of kings, for the Inquisition, for the condemnation of Galileo, and of Darwin, even for torture and slavery. From the perspective of this century, theological justification for any of the aforementioned would be difficult, even impossible.

### Theology Is Not Neutral

Theology is incomplete for yet another reason. What we usually call theology without any adjectival modifier is really European, white, middle-class, male theology. This traditional theology presumes an education, leisure to think and write, the critique of peers, and the possibility of getting one's ideas published—until recently, all the province of white, middle-class, European (and to a lesser degree, North American) males. We speak now of a variety of theologies: Black, Latin American, Asian, African, and feminist theologies, to name but a few. By using adjectives for these theologies and not also labeling the traditional theology with an adjective, the impression that is left is that only one is real theology and the others are aberrations. It masks the fact that all theologizing, as all thought, is influenced by the society in which it is produced. Inherent cultural biases are overlooked; the fact that all data is theory-laden is forgotten. It is as though traditional theology were value-free, neutral, beyond cultural exigencies, untouched by any ideology.

The *American Heritage Dictionary* defines ideology as the body of ideas reflecting the social needs and aspirations of an individual, class, or culture. There is no way to escape having an ideology; the trick is to bring the ideology of one's class or culture to consciousness, to judge it, and either affirm or reject it. Sociologists and psychologists, as well as theologians, challenge us to investigate the unexamined mind-set that contributes to and colors all our ideas; to critically examine the thinking characteristic of our culture; and to ponder the ideologies that undergird our thinking.

Everyone works out of some ideological base, whether it is articulated or not. The question, then, is not whether our cultural heritage has an impact on our thinking, but rather what kind of impact does it have and should that impact be modified in any way? Ideologies that are unexamined ordinarily operate to maintain the *status quo*. Human beings tend to be more comfortable when the circumstances of their lives are not disrupted by questioning their validity. And yet, once it is acknowledged that everyone works out of some ideological perspective, it becomes incumbent upon us to critically reflect on the ideologies prevalent in our society. More importantly, it becomes incumbent on us to question our own ideologies. The danger of ignoring the effects of ideology is that the unattended social, political, and economic assumptions will influence the theory developed, without themselves being questioned.

Theology, like history, is not neutral. It is written from a specific social foundation and either supports or challenges that foundation. An aboriginal history of the "New World" would not be a record of the glorious advance of the white race across the North American continent. The English account of the American Revolution, the Southern account of the American Civil War describe different situations than the ones I learned in school. So, too, each age theologically interprets the events of the times and either supports or challenges the political and cultural structures. The Hebrews read the hand of God in their exodus from Egypt; the early Christians reinterpreted their Jewishness in the light of the teaching of Jesus; in the fourth century, Christianity was once more reinterpreted in the light of its acceptance by the state. In our own day, the attention being paid to war and peace, the destruction of the planet, and to unjust economic systems, for instance, grows out of the concerns of this time.

Acknowledging that all theology is marked by the culture in which it develops, is not a denial of revelation. God speaks to us in the daily events of life, even as God spoke to our forebears in the events of their lives. Like the Hebrews, we follow the pillar of cloud by day and the pillar of fire by night; like the early Christians, we search the scriptures in the light of recent events to make sense of the events; like the fourth-century Christians, newly accepted by the state, we investigate the connections and disconnections between Christianity and the state. Theology is the attempt to understand our faith in the light of the events of our times and, as such, is still developing and is still incomplete.

### Liberation Theologies
The phrase "theology of liberation" was invented by Gustavo Gutierrez, generally regarded as the father of liberation theology. It is no secret that it is suspect in more conservative quarters of the church. Suspect because it is misunderstood, even as Thomas Aquinas was suspect because he was so little understood. Like Thomas, today's theologians use the knowledge available to them in the development of their theology. Thomas used the insights of Augustine and Aristotle; the liberation theologians use the insights and wisdom of sociologists, political and economic scientists, as well as psychologists.

The basic difference between traditional theology and liberation theologies is the starting point. Traditionally, theology begins with the revelation of God as known through scripture and tradition. Liberation theologians begin with the revelation of God as known through the life experience of women and men, specifically of oppressed women and men. Liberation theologies are, therefore, called theologies from below, from the life of the people. Traditional theology, on the other hand, is known as theology from above, from theories and principles, distilled from scripture and tradition. The problem with this above and below dichotomy is that "above" seems to connote that it really comes from Above, revealed by God, while "below" suggests that it really comes from Below, not from God. "Above/below" conceals the fact that all theologies develop from reflected-upon experiences of people. All involve lived experience, all involve theories and principles. It is the emphasis given on one side or the other that determines the nature of the theology developed.

Liberation theology is not only a new theology but a new way of doing theology, one which deliberately and consciously attends to and places great importance on the ideology out of which a theology develops. Liberation theology can not be done only academically. It is authenticated only when it is joined to action to eliminate injustice and violence. Because it develops out of the experience of people, liberation theology has a variety of faces. Asians, Africans, Latin Americans, Native Americans, Blacks have each experienced oppression in a distinct way; each have experienced God's abiding presence differently. Moreover, in each society, women have experienced God's presence (or absence) in radically different ways than men. The theology being developed by women in contexts of economic and political oppression is related to but not the same as the theology done by men in their various societies. It is related to but not the same as the theology done by European and American white middle-class women.

No theology is developed in a vacuum; all theology is colored by the wisdom of its day. The explicit non-neutrality of liberation theologies raises questions about the claim of neutrality of all theology. As I have already suggested, all knowledge, including theology, is colored by the age in which it is developed. Liberation theologies challenge all theology to be more aware of and more deliberate about that influence.

To claim that God is known through the experiences of the poor and oppressed in society is not to claim that the oppressed are sinless or excused from all responsibility in their lives. Nor is it to claim that dominant peoples alone are responsible for sin in society. Rosemary Radford Ruether[1] warns against a one-sided distortion that identifies the oppressed as saints and projects upon oppressors all evil and condemnation. Romanticizing the poor is a subtle form of condescension; it does not take people seriously. Black educators and religious leaders are calling our attention to the dangers inherent in lower expectations and negative identities.

In the experience of oppression, subordinate people have been victimized by their own powerlessness and have internalized the negative image assigned them by the dominant society. Horizontal violence, violence aimed at persons most like oneself, is only one of the results of this negative self identity. The anger and frustration of those who are despised is often misdirected to others who are also despised. We have only to read the crime statistics of any inner city to realize that the poor and oppressed are the primary victims of brutality and savagery. The tragic destruction and looting in inner city riots illustrate this only too well. The property and livelihood of the poor are what is destroyed; the lives of the impoverished made more difficult.

Fear of freedom, spoken of by Paulo Freire,[2] is another result of the negative identity of dominated persons. Not accustomed to autonomy and responsible decision making, subordinate peoples do not perceive themselves equal to the task of challenging oppressive situations. The move toward freedom demands the difficult task of divesting oneself of the myths which support oppressive situations. To strip away the myths which support one's life, even if these myths oppress, is to question the validity of that life. It is to bring one's very existence into question. Freedom requires accepting responsibility; but it is often easier to choose security rather than risk freedom. Besides, pleasing persons with power is often a matter of survival. Life proceeds more easily when decision making is left to them.

But in relationships of domination, the oppressor is dehumanized also. While the dehumanization is not as demeaning, dominating people are caught in a web of relationships in which they constantly need to protect themselves and their interests and in which power and prestige are valued more than relationships. Liberation theologians are concerned with creating a society and a church in which domination and subordination are eventually eliminated. They are not concerned with over-throwing the powerful and installing the subordinates in positions of power. Liberation theology is about the redefinition of power, the redefinition of relationships, and ultimately the redefinition of society.

### Feminist Liberation Theologies

Feminist theologies have common roots with other liberation theologies. Arising from and beginning with the revelation of God gleaned from the experience of women, they examine the ideologies of patriarchal society as well as their own ideologies. The experiences of women which form the starting point of feminist theology have both negative and positive aspects. Negatively, patriarchy has defined woman as less than man and has excluded her from education, health care, cultural advantages, and responsibility for the public welfare. The bible and tradition are androcentric; women have been defined primarily as complementary to and subordinate to men. Positively, feminist research has uncovered the contributions of women throughout history and the central place of women in early Christianity both of which have been ignored in a more traditional reading. To focus only on the negative would leave women without hope, on the verge of despair; to focus only on the positive would leave women naively optimistic. Feminist theologians denounce whatever is dehumanizing to women and announce the transformation of society. Denouncing and announcing are equally important to the development of any liberation theology.

Some feminists hold that Christianity can no longer speak to or for women; that it has been one of the major forces in history for exploiting women; that it is irredeemably patriarchal and therefore anti-woman. Indeed, there are indications that the persons who are leaving the Catholic Church in the greatest proportion are young well-educated women who have learned not to trust religious leaders. "If one combines confidence in church leadership and college attendance one finds that the statistically significant negative relationship between 'feminism' and church attendance is confined to those who have lower levels of confidence in religious leadership *and* who have attended college."[3] The sexist attitude of many clergy and the lack of respect for women's talents and abilities account for the lower levels of confidence.

Mary Daly is an example of such women. She was among the first and best known feminist theologian/philosophers. Daly now denounces the customs, rites, doctrines, and dogmas of Christianity as irredeemably sexist and therefore not salvific for women. She identifies herself as Post-Christian. In spite of her rejection of Christianity as inherently sexist, her questions are vital, even to those of us who have opted to remain within the Christian tradition.

### A Two-Way Conversation

In the process of articulating an alternative theology, Christian women have raised a significant question: not has Christianity anything to say to feminism, but what do Christianity and feminism have to say to one another? The conversation goes in both directions. Each critiques the other and in the process a theology which is feminist is generated. Once recognized, the oppression of women indicts the church for its support of systems which subordinate women and for its own sin of sexism. Furthermore, when the basic principles of Christianity are turned on Christianity, when they weigh and measure Christianity, they join in the indictment.

Rosemary Radford Ruether finds in scripture four prophetic and liberating themes that prefer charges against Christianity. They are: 1) God's defense and justification of oppressed people; 2) the critique of dominant systems of power; 3) the vision of the reign of God in which injustice is overcome and peace and justice prevail; and 4) the critique of ideology, or of religion, since in the context of the bible, ideology is primarily religious.[4] When these prophetic themes are applied to the history and teachings of Christianity, they often reveal theological justifications for dominant ideologies. These justifications have thus concealed the liberating message of the gospel. Both prophetic writings and the gospels proclaim advocacy for the poor and condemnations of unjust social hierarchies. Scripture denounces religious sanction for domination.

When read from the perspective of women, scripture provides the prophetic and liberating principles with which to judge the world and the church, as well as scripture itself and the interpretations of scripture through the centuries. Feminist liberation theology is not about the task of destroying or replacing traditional theology any more than the feminist movement is about the business of destroying society. The aim is to enrich the theological enterprise, to bring to it the talents, experiences, scholarship, and reflections of half the human community. The long-range hope is, of course, that feminist theology, like all liberation theologies, will no longer be necessary, will become obsolete; that it will so affect theological thought that all theologies will be colored by the principles of feminism and will explicitly draw from reflection on the lives of both women and men, both powerful and powerless.

In this regard, I am reminded of the words of John Fry:

> I propose that theologians write theology from the standpoint of the mother in Bombay (or Pittsburgh) whose child has just starved to death. She would not be theology's primary reader, and her situation would not provide theology's subject matter. But her rage and her grief would provide its angle of vision.[5]

Whether talking about the Trinity or the Incarnation, the nature of humanity or the nature of the church, we can no longer opt for the illusion of objectivism or a pseudo-neutrality. Since all theology is ideological, it is our obligation to identify our own ideology and admit the bias of our theological stance.

### Characteristics of Feminist Theology

*Praxis* By including the perspective of women, critical feminist theology provides a less inadequate way for women and men to understand Christian tradition. It provides not only theories but also strategies for assuming responsibility for the church, its structures, and its life. A good example of this kind of feminist theology comes from the National Consultation held in India in 1984. The participants discussed dowry, rape, prostitution, and the marginal roles accorded to women, even ordained women, in the churches. As a result of their reflection on scripture and the Christian tradition, the delegates issued a report to the churches of India in which "The churches were further exhorted to give a theological reinterpretation to human sexuality, and to revitalize theological education in seminaries and in sermons so as to bring about a sensitivity to the humanhood of women in an attempt to strengthen the community of men and women at the ecclesial level."[6] Reflection and action were not separated. Theologizing in the light of past and present injustices and oppressions demands conversion of sinful systems and individual commitment to the Reign of God.

*Comprehensive*   You can not be a part-time feminist; nor can you do feminist theology in a library or classroom and forget it elsewhere. Feminist theology involves praxis, action, and reflection in such a way as to be constantly renewing itself. Praxis is not the application of theory to practice; it is not applying predetermined principles to a situation. Praxis is action/reflection as one moment, not as subsequent events. Reflection upon practice leads to new questions and demands alternative actions which when reflected upon lead to new questions.... Not merely cerebral and intellectual nor merely activist and emotional, feminist theology does not deny the necessity of either. Rigorous, passionate research and intelligent, passionate participation in the transformation of the world enrich and challenge each other. Praxis is reflection-informed-by-practice and practice-informed-by-reflection. It is an ongoing process, always searching, never imagining that it has arrived at "The Truth."

*Holistic*   In its many manifestations feminist theology is holistic, avoids dichotomies and dualisms. It is inclusive, and as such, searches beyond the Christian tradition for hints of the Divine. The experience of women and the contributions of the culture as well as tradition are the loci of the revelation of God. One is likely to see Mother Jones or Maya Angelou quoted along with Thomas Aquinas. Furthermore, because they are so keenly aware of their own exclusion, feminist theologians are learning to be sensitive to those who are usually not invited to the theological conversation. Women in the developing countries and women of color in so-called advanced nations such as the United States are challenging middle-class feminist theologians and are beginning to influence their theology.

Professional theological societies are beginning to be challenged by theologians from Black, Hispanic, and Native American traditions. This is not to suggest that these challenges have accomplished a radical shift in the way most theologians think but rather that having had the spotlight turned on a culture of exclusion, theologians are more responsible for inclusion in the future.

The first wave of feminist writings came from North America and Europe, but the past few years have witnessed a torrent of writings from Latin America. Even more recently, feminist theologians from Asia and Africa have begun to contribute to the conversation. Christianity on these continents has developed in the midst of Hindu, Confucian, and Moslem societies; therefore, the experience of women has been marked by the customs and mores of those societies. The theology that is developing is of a different kind from that developed in Europe and North America. Theologians from more traditionally Christian areas struggle to include these insights and thereby enrich their own theology.[7]

*Consciously Ideological*    Feminist theology is deliberately and consciously ideological; its stated bias is the liberation of oppressed women and men from the burden of patriarchy. As such, it sees the claims and concerns of Christianity in relation to its effects on women.  In its consciously ideological stance, feminism is revisioning, reclaiming, and reconceiving.

### Feminism Is Revisioning
To revision Christianity is to see the symbols, myths, and metaphors from a new standpoint, reclaiming, in a new way, those symbols, myths, and metaphors which are life-giving, reconceiving the Christian message, bringing forth the Vision anew.

Remember the children's game where you had to find the objects hidden in a picture? There may have been cats in a tree or clowns on the roof. At first, it was difficult to see some of them, but once recognized, they did not disappear. Or think of the images in which either two profiles or a vase can be seen, or the head of an old woman or a young woman. Once you are able to find both, it is relatively easy to go back and forth, seeing both. But you cannot see both simultaneously, attending to one temporarily conceals the other. So it is with feminist thought. Feminist men and women do not lose their ability to see in the more traditional patriarchal way, but they have gained new vision and are able to see what may have been present but hidden before.

In visiting a foreign country, the novelty of scenes and customs demands our attention; if we stay for a while, we stop seeing, things become familiar. The process of becoming familiar, of course, lets us get on with life; it can be tiring being bombarded with new visions; they sap the energy and command notice. When a man or a woman becomes a feminist, nothing looks the same. After my own conversion to feminism, when I read scripture I often said, "That's new; it wasn't there the last time. Someone must have sneaked it in when I wasn't looking." Of course, it was always there. I had been unseeing. I had read the words from the perspective of the culture in which I lived and understood them from that perspective. But when my worldview changed, so did my ability to vision and revision scripture (and incidently to revise and revision *The New York Times*, television shows, and the theater). I was left with questions, surprises, and disappointments. The new view was not always comforting.

My consolation came from finding a community of women who also saw the world as I did. Without them, I might have gone mad, for a person can not be alone in holding to an alternative worldview. One needs a community. The poet Adrienne Rich has captured the feeling: "The sleepwalkers are coming awake, and for the first time this awakening has a collective reality; it is no longer such a lonely thing to open one's eyes."[8]

Revisioning also means changing or modifying the impact of certain texts. Texts which have been used against women and which foster misogyny in the church and society are being reconsidered and in some cases rejected as simply indications of the cultural biases of the author and not of divine revelation. Some texts are revisioned in the light of the questions of this century and of the extraordinary biblical research of today. Revising, revisioning is one way for feminists to remain faithful to the Christian faith, rejecting aspects that have demeaned them while holding on to what has nourished. Rich once more provides the words: "Revisioning—the act of looking back, of seeing with fresh eyes, of entering an old text for a new critical direction—is for us more than a chapter in cultural history: it is an act of survival."[9] For some women, especially poor women and women of color, survival takes on such an urgency that liberation is not the basis from which their theology develops, survival is—survival as women, survival as Christians.

*Feminist Hermeneutics* To facilitate such a revisioning, Elisabeth Schüssler Fiorenza proposes a feminist model of biblical interpretation. It is an approach to the study of scripture (and, I might add, to all theology) that begins with a hermeneutics of suspicion and progresses to a hermeneutics of proclamation, of remembrance, and of creative actualization.[10] Hermeneutics, a method of interpreting (especially used in reference to interpreting the bible), needs to be done with more of a sense of suspicion, of questioning, of disbelief even. We need to make our own the rabbinic question, "Why, Why, Why?" Why are women eliminated? Why are women blamed? Why are women described negatively? Why are women vulnerable to abuse in society and in the church? Why are women's contributions discounted? Why? Why?

Easy acceptance of the interpretations of another time does not give us adequate enough access to the scriptures. Scripture and its interpretations have been formed in and by androcentric societies. They serve to uphold and foster patriarchal values. As such, they may not be accepted uncritically but need to be critically examined in the light of the widespread oppression of women. A feminist hermeneutics of suspicion searches for connections and causes of oppression that may have been overlooked in an androcentric reading.

Patriarchal principles that oppress women must be rejected,

but it is important to remember that patriarchy is not the incarnation of evil. Like other human constructs, it is both good and
evil. Patriarchy has been the context out of which persons accomplished both good and bad in society. Writers from patriarchal societies speak of justice, of liberation, of love; they speak
of the coming of God's reign; they exalt loyalty in relationships
with others, forgiveness and love of neighbor, and fidelity to the
covenant with God. But the deficiencies of patriarchy did not allow for dominant males to apply the same principles to women
and subordinate men. What is new is that feminist theologians
are applying to women these liberating principles.

A feminist hermeneutics of proclamation recognizes that
scripture and theology are androcentric. To deny this is to deny
history. Past history need not be destroyed; scripture scholars
and theologians research the documents of the past in order to
understand the development of the faith. But everything in
scripture should not be offered for our edification. Violent and
militaristic texts ought not be proclaimed; texts upholding slavery ought not be proclaimed. Texts subjugating women ought
not be proclaimed. Sexist or patriarchal texts ought not be in-
serted in the lectionary (and where they are already present,
ought not be read at worship). They have no place in the proclamation of the Christian message. What is written, is written,
and is significant for scholars but we need not preach and teach
it as though it is theologically meaningful for contemporary society. Liturgists, educators, preachers, and pastors are developing a sensitivity to the unintended and oppressive
messages that reside in some of scripture and are not proclaiming it as the word of God.

### Feminism Is Reclaiming

An interpretation of our tradition made in the light of feminism (a feminist hermeneutics of remembrance), according to
Fiorenza, reclaims both the suffering and struggle of women in
the patriarchal Christian past and the commitment and leadership of women in the first Christian communities. This positive
and negative memory is a "dangerous memory," a "subversive
memory." Christian feminists can echo the words of Jewish theo-

logian Judith Plaskow to her sisters in religion, "Read with new questions and critical freedom, traditional sources can yield 'subversive memories' of past struggles for liberation within and against patriarchy, memories that link contemporary women to a transformative history."[11] The women in our past, our foremothers who struggled within and against patriarchy, are then the first concern of feminists who are about the work of reclaiming. Eve and Lilith, Sarah and Hagar, Mary and Mary Magdalen are but a few of the subversive memories that are inspiring feminist thinkers to transform history.

*Reclaiming symbols and metaphors*   The second concern in the process of reclaiming are the myths, symbols, and metaphors of Christianity that have functioned to maintain the subordination of women. Myths, symbols, and metaphors organize our world; they give meaning and structure to what otherwise would only be a hodge-podge of impressions. What things mean is more significant to us than what they are, and metaphors and symbols are about the meaning of things. But in order to have meaning, they must capture us, integrate us into themselves. A symbol is composed of three things: itself, what it represents, and our own psychic investment. Symbols speak to a deep part of our being and demand more than an intellectual investment. Think of the symbol of a wedding ring. Alone it is only a piece of metal, but invested with the love and fidelity of marriage, it becomes a symbol. It is significant because it has captured the human psyche.

Paul Tillich noted that "Symbols die because they can no longer produce response in the group where they originally found expression."[12] Perhaps they have to die in order that they may be reborn with new meaning. During the past few decades we have been experiencing a crisis of symbols. Part of the reason women are dislocated and alienated is that they lack a symbolic framework. The perspective of the dominant male society determines symbol systems.

Many women have internalized the patriarchal view and symbolic system that defined them only as wives, mothers, whores, mistresses, or virgins, all specifications in relation to men. Novelist Tillie Olsen calls the phenomenon a "denial of circumference" as she describes the pressure women writers experience in accepting the entrenched attitudes of society. They falsify their own range of vision, their own truth, their own voice. They deny the profound visions of women, they express their deepest truths in the character or voice of a male so that they may be heard and they proclaim that "one's sex has nothing to do with one's writing."[13] Not only are women defined from a male perspective, more importantly, they deny their own inspirations. They believe that their sex has nothing to do with the reading of symbols and metaphors and they hear and speak the language of a predominantly male society as if it were their own.

The acceptance of misogynous symbols and metaphors by women through the ages has been detrimental to both their growth and sanctity. Symbols and metaphors which do not speak to a person's experience, even though they have historical relevance, do not survive. Reflecting only on past glory and unable to touch people's lives, they die. Symbols and metaphors grow out of the heritage and present experience of a community as well as out of the personal experience of individuals who adopt them. Conversely, they provide a lens through which we see that community, through which we interpret its history, and through which we identify one another in the community.

*Reclaiming Language*   Language is of such importance that it needs to be discussed separately from other symbols. Language is an arbitrary and powerful symbol created by humans who are, in turn, created by language. Language conditions our thinking; the extent of our language is the extent of our thought. Words enable us to communicate with one another; yet, words sometimes get in the way of the message. They give us the means to speak about beauty, justice, power, and love—even of the beauty, justice, power, and love of God. At the same time, words conceal that beauty, justice, power, and love. Words both liberate and imprison us. Patriarchal language, which kept women invisible and implied that the male was the norm for the human, went for the most part unnoticed by all except the most perceptive, but we have recently become more attentive to the power of words. Religious language especially served to maintain male dominance. Elizabeth Cady Stanton, one of the first wave of feminists, wrote:

You may go over the world and you will find that every form of religion which has breathed upon this earth has degraded women.... What power is it that makes a Hindoo woman burn herself on the funeral pyre of her husband: Her religion. What holds the Turkish woman in the harem? Her religion. By what powers do the Mormons perpetuate their system of polygamy? By their religion. Man, of himself, could not do this; but when he declares, "Thus says the Lord," of course he can do it.[14]

Stanton was equally critical of the effects of Christianity on women. More than one hundred fifty years ago, she led a group of women from church when the minister preached on the first epistle of Timothy 2:12, "A woman must listen in silence and be completely submissive."[15] She knew the power of words and the powerlessness of imposed silence.

The liberation movements of the late twentieth century have forced us to become conscious that the language we use creates and reinforces the *status quo* or challenges it. The insistence of feminists concerning inclusive language has eliminated some of the invisibility of women; it has helped to redefine relationships and structures of society; it has even provided new insights into the nature of God. The United Presbyterian Church's Document, "Opening the Door" expresses it beautifully:

...our changing language about God theologically implies a change in how we perceive God and ourselves. It implies more honest translation of Scripture to eliminate distortions in language. It implies a broader concept of the Godhead beyond images of human beings. It implies appreciation and keeping alive the mystery of God. It implies an openness of the Church to a basic assumption...that language used in worship and work of the church should affirm the wholeness of God and full personhood of all.[16]

Much of the rest of this book has to do with revisioning and reclaiming the symbols, myths, and metaphors of Christianity in such a way that women and men are able to describe themselves as Christian feminists without being asked how that is possible. Christian feminist is not an oxymoron. On the contrary, I find it difficult to understand how a person can be Christian without accepting the values of reverence and care proposed by feminism.

### Feminism Is Reconceiving

The fourth element suggested by Fiorenza in the development of a feminist biblical interpretation (and theological interpretation) is imaginative articulation. Imagination is not fantasy. It is a way of thinking, a way of knowing. Imagination and reason are not enemies and must not be separated. In this regard, Black theologian Delores Williams writes, "The imagination must have equal status with reason in theological construction, so that the voices of many diverse women can speak of the God they know."[17]

Imagination brings to life through our creative powers what may have been dormant or even rejected in our tradition. Through imagination we are able to make connections, see disjointures, bridge seemingly unrelated issues, and in the process, develop a new way of seeing. We conceive of the tradition anew —conceive—in the sense of mentally appropriating it and conceive, in the sense of bringing it to new life. Having rejected what was oppressive; revised what was misunderstood; reclaimed what is ours, feminists are in a position to reconceive, to create, to contribute to the development of Christianity in a more conscious and open way than was possible in the past. The reconstruction of Christian tradition, the reconceiving of the past is accomplished by unearthing the neglected history, the untold stories, the hidden background. This requires a freeing of the imagination from sedimented images and ideas. The androcentric texts available to us, when examined through a feminist lens, afford glimpses of another parallel but submerged history. That women's Christian tradition, once recognized, reveals the misogyny of the normative sources.

Women are not the first to imaginatively recreate the tradition. Creative imagination has always been used by the church; narrative, song, liturgies, painting, and sculpture have interpreted certain aspects of the Christian tradition and ignored oth-

ers, have celebrated the contributions of some and have neglected that of others. Each age, consciously or unconsciously,
read and interpreted scripture creatively, wresting meaning
from the text that the author may not have intended or even recognized. Hints, clues, and insinuations in the text provide the
pieces of a mosaic which when creatively arranged and related
to each other yield fresh insights.

New questions exact new answers. For example, instead of
simply preaching that Paul told women to be silent in church, we
might ask, What was going on in the community that Paul dis-
approved of? Were women speaking out? Why would he have
been threatened by that? Or, why are fathers not among the hundredfold promised by Jesus? Is he saying something about patriarchy? Or, could it have been possible for Jews to celebrate
Passover, a family feast, without women and children present?
In revisioning, reclaiming, and reconceiving their Christian heritage, feminists approach that tradition with a healthy dose of
suspicion and with a determination to remember the contributions of the neglected women who have gone before us.

A hermeneutics of creative imagination allowed Marjorie
Proctor-Smith,[18] for example, to reconceive the nameless woman
who anointed the head of Jesus in such a way that we see her as
if for the first time. The content and context of the story are liturgical. The woman performs the liturgical act of anointing, one
which prophets performed in the making of kings. It is also a political act that challenges both religious and political powers. A
baptismal motif is also present, anointing with oil being an expression of the Messianic priesthood used in ancient baptismal
rites. While this forgotten woman could be used along with John
who baptized in the Jordan, she is not. Her story has been mu-
tilated, and she along with it, so that her image is that of a sinner
groveling for forgiveness.

> The story of the forgotten woman and her liturgical act
> stands as a paradigm of the failure of the church in its lit-
> urgy not only to remember women and their liturgical-
> prophetic deeds, but also women's memories. For the
> church not only failed to remember the woman's name; it

also failed to remember the significance of the event, as, for example, Luke's redaction of the story shows.[19]

In the Jewish tradition, midrashic commentaries on scripture have extracted religious significance from a text. Believing that the scriptures held limitless meaning, rabbis wrote troublesome passages forward in the light of their own concerns. Some have enriched Jewish women's religious practice; some have been used against women. Today, both Christian and Jewish women are using midrashim to imagine and articulate their religious understanding of their history and tradition. Judith Plaskow's midrash on Lilith (see chapter seven of this book) transforms a demeaning myth about women into a challenging, inspiring one. Plaskow explains that in writing women into Jewish history, feminists are extending the realm of a potentially usable Jewish past and establishing a Jewish community that can be a community of both women and men. "Women's experiences increase the domain of Jewish resources on which we can draw in recreating Judaism in the present, inspiring us to find our own forms of expression as the women and men of the past found theirs."[20] Christians can say "Amen" to that.

This creative articulation is not imaginative fantasy but is rooted in the critical process of reclaiming our heritage. Creative imagination when done by women helps us to realize that much of what passes for traditional teaching is the result of creative imagination of male theologians, preachers, and liturgists through the ages. Tradition is not an account of what really happened but of what is remembered. We are all creators of tradition, traditioners, rememberers.

Fiorenza's book *But She Said* adds another dimension to the reading of scripture. She insists that the rhetorical practices of the evangelists shaped and formed biblical stories to foster particular beliefs and practices in the communities for which they were writing. A rhetorical model of interpretation looks behind the words to discover the author's aim in writing, the persuasive strategies used, and the point of view represented. It seeks to discover how and why the author constructed the story in a certain way and to uncover the values that were being proposed. It asks what symbolic worlds and moral universes the author was attempting to produce.

A critical feminist interpretation attends not only to the domination of women but to interlocking systems of racism, classism, colonialism, and sexism. Kyriocracy, the rule of the Lord, rather than simply patriarchy, the rule of the father, is rooted in scripture as well as in interpretations through the ages.

Fiorenza advises that women read the bible "against the grain" in order to unearth the rhetorical practice of the authors. Finally, a critical feminist interpretation seeks to discover what the bible does to a person who submits to the author's worldview.

*Broadening Feminist Concerns*   Until recently, "women" was used by white European or American women to describe their context. Third world feminists have challenged that understanding and have begun to speak from social contexts that challenge such a narrow perspective. While much of what appears in this book is the fruit of reflection on the theology developed by North American and European feminists, I have tried to learn from Black and Latina feminists and to be sensitive to their concern that middle-class white women not universalize their experience and insights.

Feminist concern extends beyond human creation. Deep connections between the abuse of women and the abuse of nature have colored the recent works of theologians like Sallie McFague, Rosemary Radford Ruether, and Elizabeth Johnson.[21] I will discuss the connection between ecological concerns and Christian feminism in chapter nine.

### Questions for Reflection

1. How has your theology changed through the years because of your experiences?

2. Does the experience of women have something different to add to the theological enterprise? What would that be?

3. How might we become more aware of the revelation of God in the lives of other persons and other cultures?

4. Is a hermeneutics of suspicion (asking why, why, why?) an appropriate way to approach scripture and theology? Why or why not?

## Endnotes

1. Rosemary Radford Ruether, *Liberation Theology: Human History Confronts Christian History and American Power* (New York: Paulist Press, 1972) 10-16.

2. Paulo Freire, *Pedagogy of the Oppressed* (New York: Herder and Herder, 1971) 31-32.

3. Andrew Greeley and Mary G. Durkin, *Angry Catholic Women* (Chicago: Thomas More Press, 1984).

4. Rosemary Radford Ruether, *Sexism and God-Talk: Toward a Feminist Theology* (Boston: Beacon Press, 1983) 24-33.

5. John Fry, "The Great Apostolic Blunder Machine:" *Harper Magazine*, 74-75.

6. Stella Faria, "A Reflection on the National Consultation: Ecumenicity of Women's Theological Reflections," in *Towards a Theology of Humanhood: Women's Perspectives* edited by Aruna Gnanadason (Delhi: All India Council of Christian Women, 1986) 2. The AICCW, an association of theologically trained women, organized the conference.

7. See, for instance, *The Will to Arise: Women, Tradition and the Church in Africa* edited by Mercy Amba Oduyoye and Musimbi R.A. Kanyoro (Maryknoll: Orbis Books, 1992); *Through Her Eyes: Women's Theology from Latin America* edited by Elsa Tamez (Maryknoll, Orbis Books, 1989), and *With Passion and Compassion: Third World Women Doing Theology* edited by Virginia Fabella, M.M. and Mercy Amba Oduyoye (Maryknoll: Orbis Books, 1989).

8. Adrienne Rich, "When We Dead Awaken: Writing as Re-Vision" in *Adrienne Rich's Poetry* edited by Barbara Charlesworth Gelpi and Albert Gelpi (New York: W.W. Norton, 1975) 90.

9. Ibid., 90.

10. See Elisabeth Schüssler Fiorenza, *Bread, Not Stone* (Boston: Beacon: 1984) and *But She Said: Feminist Practices of Biblical Interpretation* (Boston: Beacon Press, 1992).

11. Judith Plaskow, *Standing Again at Sinai: Judaism from a Feminist Perspective* (San Francisco: Harper & Row, 1990) 15.

12. Paul Tillich, *Dynamics of Faith* (New York: Harper & Row, 1967) 43.

13. Tillie Olsen, *Silences* (New York: Delacorte Press, 1978) 249-250.

14. Quoted in Susan B. Anthony and Ida Husted Harper, eds., *The History of Woman Suffrage* Vo.1 4. (Indianapolis: The Hollenbeck Press, 1902) 60.

15. Related to Mary Jo Weaver, *New Catholic Women: A Contemporary Challenge to Traditional Religious Authority* (San Francisco: Harper &

Row, 1985) 145.

16. "The Power of Language Among the People of God and the Language About God: 'Opening the Door'" (New York: The United Presbyterian Church in the U.S.A.: 1975) 4. See also "Words That Hurt and Words That Heal" (Nashville: United Methodist Publishing House, 1985); "Women and Liturgical Language" in *Women and the Church* Kit prepared by the Canadian Conference of Catholic Bishops (Ottawa: CCCB Publications Service, 1984).

17. Delores Williams in *Immaculate and Powerful* edited by Clarissa W. Atkinson, Constance H. Buchanan, and Margaret R. Miles (Boston: Beacon, 1985) 107.

18. Marjorie Proctor-Smith, *In Her Own Rite: Constructing Feminist Liturgical Tradition* (Nashville, Abingdon, 1990) 38-39 and 57-58.

19. Ibid., 39. Luke is the only one of the four evangelists who calls the woman a sinner. See chapter eight for more on this prophetic woman.

20. Judith Plaskow, *Standing Again*, 52.

21. See Sallie McFague, *Models of God: Theology for an Ecological, Nuclear Age* (Philadelphia: Fortress, 1987); Rosemary Radford Ruether, *Gaia and God: An Ecofeminist Theology of Earth Healing* (New York: HarperCollins, 1992) and Elizabeth Johnson, *Women, Earth and the Creator Spirit* (New York: Paulist Press, 1993).

# 2

# Images of God

The inscription on the tomb of Cardinal John Henry Newman reads "The name that can be named is not the name." Simone Weil put it another way:

> There is a God. There is no God. What is the problem? I am quite sure that there is a God in the sense that I am sure that my love is no illusion. I am quite sure that there is no God in the sense that I am sure that there is nothing which resembles what I can conceive when I say that word.[1]

After acknowledging that God is beyond anything that we may say or think or believe about the Deity, we will follow the example of centuries of theologians and proceed to speak to the issue of God in this chapter. Much of what appears here we owe to the work that is being developed by feminist theologians regarding God language. I will discuss how even God has been, and unfortunately still is, used as a tool for the oppression of many, especially women. Then, I will turn attention to the Christian doctrine *par excellence*, the Trinity, as it is being conceived today in a form that is more consonant with feminist principles. Finally, attention will be paid to some newly-discovered old metaphors that may be significant for twentieth-century peoples in their conversation about God.

### You Are Not God

We do fear being iconoclasts. And with good reason; it is not a role to be taken lightly. Suppose the god we no longer believe in and who we are dismissing is God. Suppose the culture, including religion, is right in its presentation of what the "Supreme Being" is like. Such thoughts can paralyze us into uncritical compliance with what we intuit to be inadequate. Confronting images of God is fearsome, yet it is a task that cannot be shunned. There is no virtue in fidelity to lesser gods when our own experience, the experience of others, the challenge of artists and thinkers, and the contributions of theologians force the question upon us. We must ask who is the God we do not believe in.

Mary Daly,[2] almost twenty years ago, encouraged people to dethrone false deities: the God of the stop-gap, the God of other-worldliness, and the judgmental God who confirms the rightness of the reigning system. I think Daly was not speaking of three false gods but of three manifestations of the same god who is not God. The god of the gap who promises rewards and punishments and who judges sin by the norms of the prevailing culture is the god who maintains the status quo and who keeps persons in their proper place in the structure of that status quo. The power of the god of other-worldliness is asserted in this way: The will of this god is beyond our comprehension and so we can only explain the unexplainable by saying, "It is for the best. It is God's will." Or we assure one another that unnecessary suffering in this life will be balanced by rewards in the next. This is the god who kept slaves submissive.

The third manifestation of this patriarchal god is the god who judges sin according to the norms of the powerful and dominant in society. The laws and regulations that govern and confine women's lives were imposed by dominant males. Women have had no say in them. These remarks are not to be construed to mean that suffering has nothing to do with eternal life. On the contrary. But some suffering is dehumanizing, degrading, demonic, sinful. It ought not be tolerated. A god who supports such "dirty suffering" is not God.

The rejection of this god is not a call to anarchy, but rather a challenge to free ourselves, one another, and even God from the bonds of a triumphalistic patriarchy. Feminists, in their search for models, metaphors, and images for God are seeking to deepen their relationship with the deity, not eliminate it.

### Naming God

What both Newman and Weil are saying is that whatever we say about God cannot be understood to be a description or definition of the Deity. The best we can do is acknowledge that we are speaking about the One who is Sublime Mystery and that our speech is Earth-bound, halting, finite. Whatever our words do in reference to God, they do not name the Holy One. We cannot bestow a name on God, for naming something or someone gives us power over that one. We have only to look to the scriptures to understand that naming is a source of power. Adam's power and dominance over the rest of creation is signaled in his right to name the animals. Recall, too, the fairy tale of Rumpelstiltskin, how the queen had to find out the name of the little man so that she could have power over him and be reunited with her child. Once she could sing out the name, she was no longer powerless.

"God" is not God's name. The three letters, g-o-d, are one way we humans attempt to communicate with one another about the mystery of what has classically been called "the Supreme Being." When human awareness awoke to the realization that there was more to life than appeared to the senses, our ancestors imagined a host of gods who lived and loved much as humans but on another plane. They made war and they made love, they birthed new gods and killed off old ones. Our forebears identified other gods besides the gods of mythology; the forces of nature, the sun, sky, and ocean, volcanoes, and mountains were recognized as having power beyond human ability. They were sometimes worshipped, if not as gods themselves, then as the dwelling place of the gods. In a slow process, over the course of centuries, one people grew in the understanding of God's oneness and of

God's relationship with them.

### The Relational God

The Israelites recognized in the sufferings and joys of the people the abiding presence of God. The amazing insight they had is that the gods who were thought to exist in another sphere or the gods who abided in nature were not God. The experience of a God who was involved in their history, who intervened on their behalf, who made covenants with them and kept these covenants, no matter what, slowly led Israel from polytheism to monotheism. There is one God, no other is God. They used many symbols, metaphors, and analogies taken from nature, from human structures, and human relationships in trying to explain to one another what the experience of this God was. These human symbols, metaphors, and analogies speak of the relationship between Israel and God. The God of Abraham and Sarah, of Jacob and Rebecca, of Isaac and Rachel and Leah, is not a God indifferent to and detached from the people. Their God is not a God revealed only in nature but a God of history who acts in and through Israel, a God who is involved with and committed to the people.

Scripture records that when Moses asked who it was who spoke to him he received the reply, "Yahweh," traditionally understood as "I am who am." This translation transmits a connotation of a God who is not only complete in the Divine Being Itself, but is also rather distant and uninvolved. It does not suggest relationship either within the Godhead or with humanity. An alternative translation, more in line with recent theological developments, renders the Latin, "Adsum," and the English "I shall be with you as Who I Am."[3] The sense here is of a God who is involved with, engaged with, absorbed with the people of Israel. It better carries our belief that God is related to us and acts on our behalf.

If Christians had to decide on only one category for discussing God that category would be, I believe, relational. Two recent award winning books, *God With Us* by Catherine Mowry LaCugna and *She Who Is* by Elizabeth Johnson, open new avenues by which to approach the mystery of a relational God, a

God who is known to us as Trinity.[4] The Trinity is not about a magical threeness but about the relation between the Father, the Word, and the Spirit. This revelation is most profound in Jesus who in his life, death, and resurrection is the self-revelation of God. The incarnation, ministry, death, and resurrection of Jesus reveal insights into the very life of the Trinity. It is revealed in Jesus and has to do with salvation history. It has to do with Christology (the theoretical study of Jesus Christ) and with Pneumatology (the theoretical study of the Spirit).

In the historic life of Jesus, God assumed a human history and experienced the world as human. Human history became God's own history. "Through [Jesus Christ's] human history the Spirit who pervades the universe becomes concretely present in a small bit of it. In a word, Jesus is Emmanuel, God with us."[5] God did not suspend being God in the incarnation. Nor did God suspend being God in the passion and death of Jesus. The idea of impassibility, not being subject to suffering, has been rigidly and literally interpreted so that it eventually came to stand for a God who was insensible and untouched by the agony and oppression of women and men. Our loving God is a God who is in pain with us, who grieves for us, who suffers in and through us.

The life of Jesus and his teachings reveal who God is. The liberating message of Jesus, his inclusive table community with room for the outcast of society and his fidelity to his mission even to death, impart some hint of what God is like; enough of a hint, in fact, that John could write, "God is Love." The life, mission, death, and resurrection of Jesus announce that in God's very Being, God is a lover of humankind.

The dogma of the Trinity is also made manifest in the workings of the Holy Spirit in our world. Though involved in the on-going creation of the universe and in the constant renewal of the face of Earth, the Spirit has been called the forgotten God. Perhaps it is because the Spirit is so present to us that we lose awareness. Like the air that we breathe, the Spirit is around, before, and in us. But also like the air that we breathe, the Spirit is often taken for granted. The Spirit of God saturates the universe. In loving relationships; in the struggle for justice and truth; in the joys and the pains of life, the Spirit lives.

It is not always easy to recognize the Spirit. Even some translators of scripture have trouble with seeing the Spirit at work. In
the first chapter of Genesis, they speak of a mighty wind from
God that swept over the face of the waters. Other translators recognize that it is the Spirit of God that swept over the face of the
waters. While some people see only wind and air, trees and
flowers, pets and persons, love and truth, justice and peace, others are able to recognize the Spirit and are thus able to speak of
the mystery we call God. "The Spirit is the living God present
throughout the world and in the struggle of human history. That
being so, whatever is said about the Spirit is in fact language
about the mystery of God."[6]

The God whom Jesus revealed in his life and death is a triune
God whose very essence is to be related; the God whom the
Spirit manifests in relationship with all creation is triune—
related not simply with creatures but related in the Godhead itself. Being God is being related. God's being is active, vibrant,
dynamic, productive. LaCugna writes, "The incomprehensible
God *is* God by sharing, bestowing, diffusing, expressing Godself.
The gift of existence and grace that God imparts to the world is
not produced by efficient causality, largely extrinsic to God; the
gift is nothing other than God's own self."[7]

In an earlier article, LaCugna explains "God's nature might be
to-be, but we cannot know by reason alone what such a to-be is
like. On the other hand, we can know through revelation what
God's to-be is like, namely, it is a relational to-be."[8] God's relationship with Israel, God's self-revelation in the life, death, and
resurrection of Jesus, both reveal the relationality of God. God's
constant presence with us reveals God as relational.

This relational to-be we express as the doctrine of the Trinity.
It may be that most Christians do not really believe in a relational monotheism, but rather are numerical monotheists, the
classic explanations of the doctrine of the Trinity being too abstract and esoteric for most. Moreover, "persons" does not carry
the same intent for us psychologizing people as it did for Greek
philosophy. The work that is now being developed in reconceiving the triune God avoids undue focus on language like
three persons, hypostasis, procession, in favor of the language of

relationality. Listen to the words of Johnson. "The mutual co-inherence, the dancing around together of Spirit, Wisdom, and Mother; or of mutual Love, Love from Love, and unoriginate Love; or of the three divine persons—this defines who God is as God."[9] It may be that the classical "one nature, three persons" formula does not provide the best insight into the triune God's relationality for people today.

The doctrine of the Trinity is not just a way of explaining how God relates to humanity (the economic Trinity); the doctrine of the Trinity is also an attempt to explain how God relates to God (the immanent Trinity). As the doctrine of the Trinity developed in the East, the emphasis was on the activity of the three Persons in human history; in the West, following Augustine, it was on the one Divine nature which subsists in the Father, the Son, and the Spirit. We cannot, of course, comprehend the intradivine relationship by reason alone, but only, and especially, as it is revealed to us through the human/Divine relationship. "The trinitarian symbol radically affirms the hope that God really is in accord with what has been mediated through experience, in other words, that Sophia-God corresponds to herself in bedrock fidelity."[10]

### Extra-Rational Language for the Relational God

Scriptural references to God fall into four types: They are literal designations, names for God, personifications, and metaphors.[11] Literal language about God is that language which names how Israel perceived God's presence in its history. God was a Liberator, a Covenant maker, a Restorer. The terms are literal in the sense that they describe who and what God was in the life of Israel; they also contrasted Israel's God with the many deities of neighboring tribes. While these designations tell us something about God, they also tell us something about the Israelites. The Israelites were a people who saw in their history the action of God; they interpreted their own social, cultural, and political life as somehow touched by the hand of the Eternal One. They recognized Divinity not only in the cosmos but in everyday human life. God was not just a God of nature but a God of history.

Searching for a name for God, we discover only "Yahweh"

(YHWH), the enigmatic name God revealed to Moses. Among the personifications of God that we inherit from Israel, two that are feminine are Wisdom and Shekinah.

*Wisdom*   Of Wisdom we read:

> The Lord begot me, the firstborn of God's ways
> the forerunner of God's prodigies of long ago;
> From of old I was poured forth, at the first, before
> the earth.
> When there were no depths, I was brought forth,
> when there were no fountains or springs of water;
> Before the mountains were settled in place,
> before the hills, I was brought forth...
> Then was I beside God as an artisan
> I was God's delight day by day
> Playing before God all the while,
> playing on the surface of God's Earth;
> And I found delight in the children of Earth.
>                        Prv 8: 22-25, 30-31

Wisdom is presented in the late Hebrew scriptures as a feminine aspect or expression of divine activity yet "despite the rich potential for the development of a feminine God-image which these personifications offered to the Jewish imagination, the divine feminine was severely repressed in the interests of safeguarding the oneness and transcendence of God."[12] It may be hard for us who have such a long and strong tradition of monotheism to understand a world in which the idea had to be defended and protected so vigilantly. Another indication of Israel's watchfulness to avoid any trace of polytheism is the imagery of the mystical marriage as a metaphor for describing the relationship between YHWH and Israel. If that relationship was a spousal one, then YHWH could not have a divine consort like the gods of the Greeks. God is one.

In the gospels, Wisdom is revealed in the foolishness of Christ's preference for the sinner, the outcast, the weak. When Jesus was accused of being a glutton and a drunkard, a friend of tax collectors and sinners, we are told, "God's wisdom is vindicated by all who accept it" (Lk 7:35). Paul gives witness to the impact of the Wisdom literature on the early church. He writes that the crucifixion is a stumbling block to the Jews and an absurdity to the Gentiles but "to those who are called, Jews and Greeks alike, Christ is the power of God and the Wisdom of God" (1 Cor 1:24). Further on, Paul writes of this Wisdom, "Eye has not seen, ear has not heard, nor has it so much as dawned on humanity what God has prepared for those who loved God" (1 Cor 2:9). The influence of the Wisdom literature on the Christian community is also evident in the opening words of the prologue to John's gospel. "In the beginning was the Word and the Word was in God's presence and the Word was God. Through him all things came into being, and apart from him nothing came to be" (Jn 1:1-3). "Sophia-Wisdom," with God before all things were made, has been transmuted into *Logos* (Word), and it is thought that one of the reasons for this is that the femaleness of Sophia may have been thought to be inappropriate when applied to the male Jesus.

*Shekinah* This other feminine personification of God's presence means "to dwell." It refers to the mysterious ways that the Divine presence was recognized by the Israelites, such as the cloud that covered the mountain when Moses spoke to God, the pillar of cloud by day, and the pillar of fire by night. Shekinah represents the mysterious presence of God in the things of the earth. Shekinah is another way of speaking of the Spirit among us.

Like the Israelites we, too, need literal language, personifications, and metaphors that give us hints about the God in whom we place our trust. We find that in our day the literal terms Israel used are still appropriate for us in our conversations about the Holy One. Our God is indeed Liberator, Covenant maker, and Restorer. These titles, especially that of Liberator, have become especially precious to liberation theologians who understand that God is on the side of the poor and oppressed and engages in liberation and restoration on their behalf. Our God is a God who keeps promises, who does not break the covenants made with humanity, but is constant in fidelity. We need to find the wisdom of God in the folly of this twentieth century.

The two terms of personification, Wisdom and Shekinah, may

also represent our awareness of the presence of God in our lives. We must learn to become aware of the "pillars of cloud and of fire" that illumine our path toward God. If clouds and fire can demonstrate God's presence with us, if all of creation can sing of God's abiding nearness, how much more the events of our times, the lives of women and men? It is not that personifications make God present, but that through them we can become aware of the already constant, faithful companionship of God in our lives and our world.

### Metaphors For the Divine

To help understand metaphoric God-language, let us turn our attention to the nature of metaphors. Metaphors connect, by way of comparison, two things that share something in common. However, really good metaphors have enough discontinuity that there is an element of surprise or shock when we first hear them. "Good metaphors shock," writes Ian Barbour, "they bring unlike together, they upset conventions, they involve tensions, they are implicitly revolutionary."[13] It is interesting to note that the metaphors that have been adopted by the liberation theologians to describe the experience of the oppressed—exodus, crucifixion, and resurrection—upset convention, involve tensions, and have proven revolutionary. They are good metaphors because they bring traditional Christian symbols and the lives of the poor into conversation.

Metaphors provide connections with similar concepts and ideas. They organize our thoughts, and in this process emphasize some details while suppressing others. For example, the Miss America contest has been described as the crowning of a queen. It has also been described as a cattle auction. Different metaphors send different messages. Metaphors also involve an interchange of meanings between the two terms. Each term says something about the other; meaning is transferred in both directions. We think new thoughts about each of the terms, even though we are primarily interested in the principal term. The metaphor, "War is hell," for example, tells us something about the principal term, war, but it also implies something about our understanding of hell. Each term affects the other. It was this mutual alteration that Mary Daly referred to when she claimed that because God is thought of as male, the male is thought of as God.[14] She reminds us that the metaphors we use for God profoundly affect the way we define ourselves. They determine, in part, how we perceive ourselves. The exclusive use of male references to God denies women an experience common to men. They do not have their sexual identity validated as being in the image and likeness of God. It is only through denying her sexuality or focusing on the transcendence of God over sexual identity that a woman may recognize herself as being in the image and likeness of God. The close association of males and God in language and in the structures and rituals of major religions divinize maleness at the expense of both God and women. According to Anne Carr:

> The idol of a male divinity in heaven issues in a divinizing of male authority, responsibility, power, and holiness on earth, despite avowals of religious leaders about women's equality. For the symbolism is so deeply embedded in Christian theology, church structure, and liturgical practice that the Christian imagination unconsciously absorbs its destructive and exclusionary messages from childhood on.[15]

Boys grow up with the expectation that they will acquire power, authority, and responsibility, that they will be involved in public issues. When this does not happen they perceive themselves as failures; when girls do not attain power, authority, or involvement in public life they do not think that it implies any failure on their part. Quite the contrary, women have been found to have a much greater fear of just such "masculine" expectations. Margaret Mead suggested that men are demasculinized by failure and women are defeminized by success.

But metaphors change; they take on new meanings with new experiences. Metaphors that were not recognized before, may now have taken on significance for us, and those that were valued in another age may not carry the same weight now. Some metaphors simply lose the ability to express the wisdom of an age, and they die. Recall that Tillich tells us, "Symbols die because they can no longer produce response in the group where they originally found expression."[16] We may say the same of metaphors. Metaphors that conveyed powerful images in the past are not always powerful in the present. Joanmarie Smith, for example, suggests that Lord, King, and Warrior are terms that no longer carry the same meaning as in the past. We Americans have declared that we will have no king; what we know of kings has more to do with fairy tales than with our lived experience. Likewise the metaphor Warrior God may have suggested to earlier generations that they ought to rely on God rather than arms. Perhaps we ought to avoid the warrior texts because "the subversion of militarism they convey seems too subtle for us at this time."[17] Rejecting certain metaphors is an acknowledgment that our ideas about God have changed; even more, that our experience of God must be respected. To propose that what made sense at another time and place no longer speaks to and of our experience is not to deny God but simply to acknowledge that language is part of life.

Reconceiving images rather than rejecting them out of hand and attempting to create new ones may be the more powerful way. As a people, we have already made a psychic commitment to traditional Christian symbols. They speak to our communal memories and they elicit an emotional and religious response. They have provided and may continue to provide a context for the incorporation of newer insights. As an example, the painting of "The Peasants of Solentiname" redefines the crucifixion in its depiction of the *Christus* on the cross as a peasant, emaciated and broken, with the people of the town gathered around him. This image could not be further from the one of Christ the King on the cross in royal or priestly robes with a jeweled crown on his head.

Or we might recall the sculpture of the Christa which elicited so much controversy when it was exhibited at the Cathedral of St. John the Divine. To picture a woman bleeding, suffering, and crucified redefines the oppression of women in terms that have sunk deep into the Christian psyche. That particular redefinition was very difficult for some to accept. Yet, it was that redefinition that encouraged many women to new theological and religious insights.

The anthropomorphic metaphors we use for Divinity suggest that there is something in human experience that may give a tiny glimpse of what God may be like; that dissimilarities between God and humans are not so striking as to invalidate the similarities. Father, Mother, Lord, King, Shepherd...each is a metaphor that tells us something about God, but at the same time hides something about God. What Father reveals, King does not; what Mother reveals, Shepherd does not. Metaphors are not definitions or even descriptions; they always limp a little. Because metaphors both reveal and conceal, it is a kind of idolatry to use only one metaphor for God. To do so implies that we have captured what God is. We have boxed God in, so to speak. We have named God. The first reason then to multiply our metaphors for God is to acknowledge that God is beyond anything we may say. It is a reminder of the transcendent nature of the Divinity and also of our own fragile humanity.

We have seen that good metaphors involve similarities and discontinuities; they reveal and conceal at the same time; they interchange meanings from one element to the other. As already noted, really good metaphors shock us when we first hear them. It is the very shock value that may be one of the best by-products of using female images and metaphors for God. This shock of hearing "she" raises questions not only about "she" but also about "he." I am still amused by the look of consternation when someone hears "God, she" for the first time. Often the shock moves quickly to a denial of that metaphor. It is as though it is too risky to think through the implications.

### The Metaphor of Father/Mother

To speak of God as Father is to say that there is something so wonderful about fathers and fatherhood that the word "Father" is not inappropriate when applied to God. Speaking *only* in terms of Father is the problem. The Hebrew scriptures use the Father image in reference to God about a dozen times. (There is a problem in coming up with an exact number since Catholics, Protestants, and Jews do not entirely agree on all of the books of the bible they accept.) Father is, however, a pivotal image for Jesus. One has only to check any concordance of the bible to ap-

preciate the centrality of God as Father in the life and teaching of
Jesus. A few will suffice to illustrate the point: "All things have
been delivered to me by my Father" (Mt 11:27, Lk 10:22); "Who
does not honor the Son does not honor the Father who sent him"
(Jn 5:23). And in his agony, "Abba, Father, all things are possible
for you; remove this cup from me; yet not what I will but what
you will" (Mk 14:36), and "Father, forgive them for they know
not what they do" (Lk 23:34). And finally, "Father, into thy
hands I commend my spirit" (Lk 23:46).

What is significant is that the image of Father is not one that
suggests social distance as do King, Master, and Lord; it is one
that speaks not of the measureless power and transcendence of
God, but rather of presence and immanence; "...especially in the
term 'Abba,' it conveys a nearness, an intimacy which may have
shocked Jesus' contemporaries. Concerning its initial sub-
versiveness, it is ironic to see 'Father' pressed into the service of
hierarchy."[18]

When it was believed that all life was contained in the father's
seed which was planted in the mother's womb to be nurtured,
"Father" had an even more profound implication than it does today. All life came from the father; all life came from God. God
and fathers appeared to have more in common than God and
mothers since it was believed that mothers made no contribution
to the creation of new life. Modern scientific discoveries have
changed that notion of fatherhood and in doing so have altered
our notion of God as Father. We must remember Father is not
God's name, nor does it exhaust the attributes of God that have
been revealed to us over the course of human history.

By the same token, Mother has something to say about what
God may be like, but God's name is not Mother either. It would
be a mistake, I believe, to use the image of God as Mother to reinforce society's expectations of the good mother: one who never
thinks of herself, is always there, is unconditionally accepting,
wholly centered on the child, and who washes the dishes and
makes the beds besides! Following Thomas Aquinas's lead, perhaps the best we can say is, "God is Father; God is not Father,
God is not not Father...God is Mother; God is not Mother; God is
not not Mother."

Janet Morley has an interesting theory on the resistance of both women and men to the image of God the Mother. While mother, on the one hand, suggests tenderness, compassion, nurturing, and affection, it also suggests a relationship in which we were absolutely helpless at the hands (and the body) of a woman. Mothers, or those who act as mothers, were the source of all contentment, pleasure, security, and satisfaction. But mothers were also the ones who weaned us from that pleasure and satisfaction, a denial that to a child may have seemed arbitrary. Mothers were not only the fulfillment of our childish desires but also the focus of some of our earliest frustrations. Moreover, becoming adult has to do with a growing independence from the Mother figure (male or female); few of us wish to return to a childish dependence. "Perhaps we fear that to name our Mother in God would stir some of the painful resentments we would rather not feel towards our creator. God as 'she' could get under our skin."[19]

We have only to pick up the daily paper with accounts of child abuse and neglect to realize that either Father or Mother may be the worst metaphor for some children and for some adults. Abusive parents are not a new phenomenon. While it appears that there are many more children today who are abused, it may be we are only now admitting the dirty secret of so many homes. The number of men and especially women of all ages from twenties to eighties who are seeking help from the consequences of an abused childhood staggers the imagination. It is one of the aspects of family life we would rather keep hidden.

Moreover, "parental images stress the characteristics of compassion and acceptance as well as guidance and discipline, but they cannot express mutuality, maturity, cooperation, responsibility, or reciprocity."[20] Parental images may be consoling and nurturing and as such are vital models for our relationship with God. But thinking of God only in terms of Father and Mother may unwittingly foster both a lack of responsibility toward the world and a dependence that inhibits maturity. It is an impossible stance for those who stand with the 1971 International Synod of Catholic Bishops in believing that "Action on behalf of justice and participation in the transformation of the world fully appear to us as a constitutive dimension of the preaching of the Gospel, or in other words, of the Church's mission for the redemption of the human race and its liberation from every oppressive situation."[21] Being a Christian, relating to the God of Jesus, is not the task of the immature of any age.

### God the Friend

Images, metaphors, and symbols that no longer speak to people's experience die. Other, more relevant images, symbols, and metaphors arise out of the experience of the community. One metaphor that appears to be doing just that is "Friend." Friendship is more inclusive than parenthood. We can be friends with people who are quite different from us, people who come from another culture, who may speak another language. But we may also become friends with parents, sisters, brothers, aunts, uncles, and cousins. It includes both our natural family and the extended family of all humanity.

It may even be said that all relationships strive toward friendship or they wither. Mothers and fathers who have become friends with their adult children find richness they never imagined when the relationship was one of parent-and-child. Siblings who are friends know that my sister/my friend or my brother/my friend blesses the sister and brother relationship in wonderful ways. The tragedy of wives and husbands who are not friends needs no comment. No matter what the original relationship, it is ennobled by a move toward friendship.

Sallie McFague has spun out for us the ramifications of using the metaphor of friend for God in her books *Metaphorical Theology* and *Models of God.*[22] In the first, she makes a case for an understanding of God as personal friend and in the second, she speaks of God as friend of creation, friend of Earth. There is biblical tradition supporting the image of God as friend. After all, Yahweh called Abraham "my friend" (Is 41:8), and Jesus told his disciples that he would not call them servants but friends (Jn 15:15). Jesus was the friend of sinners (Mt 11:19), and in the end he laid down his life for his friends (Jn 15:13).

What aspects of friendship might apply to the Divinity? First of all, friendship is gratuitous. It is pure gift. Friends have no legal rights over or responsibility for one another. They cannot be forced to pay another's bills; they have no right to property not specifically given them by gift or in a will. Third cousins twice removed who have never known a person have more legal rights than a close friend.

What friends give or share is gift, not formal duty. True friends do not demand or command things of one another. They do not even demand love. Indeed they cannot. Is not this a fitting way in which to describe one's relationship with God? We do not love God because we have been commanded to do so. We respond to the generous self-giving love of God by a love of our own. We can not claim any favors or special treatment from God because we call God friend, but we can trust and expect the loving treatment one friend graciously shares with another. On the other hand, God cannot force us to be a friend. Our love is our gift to God given freely.

If we think of God as friend, sorrow for sin takes on new meaning. If you have ever had the misfortune of really hurting a good friend, you may still remember the pain and the sense of loss that you experienced. You know what it is to be truly sorry, to have a firm resolution to never hurt your friend again. You are aware how tenuous friendships can be and how many friendships are irrevocably severed because the relationship has been strained, because a person is incapable of expressing sorrow for hurting the other, or because the hurt party is incapable of forgiveness. If your friendship survived, you certainly can still taste the sheer delight of forgiveness.

Forgiveness takes on different meanings when we think of God as friend. Robert Frost's "Home is where they have to take you in, no matter what" suggests that our family has more of an obligation to forgive us than others. Historical evidence and statistics suggest that the old saying may be more of a romantic notion than a true description of reality. Families are not always forgiving, yet they remain technically family. But in order to remain friends, forgiveness must be part of the web of the relationship. People make mistakes, people hurt others, people sometimes do terrible things. We are among those people who make mistakes, hurt others, and do terrible things. We are often in need of forgiveness. But the forgiveness between friends is only a glimmer of the forgiveness we can expect from God—forgiveness, not because we deserve it, but as sheer gift, absolute grace.

When we think of God as friend, we begin to look differently at prayer, too. In friendship, communication is required to keep the relationship alive; more than that, communication is demanded of us by our own need to share our joys and sorrows with those we love and trust, and to be present to them in their moments of joy or sorrow. We are impelled by our own love to reach out to someone in peak moments of our lives, and that someone is usually a close friend. What this tells us about the nature of prayer with our God as Friend is obvious.

The metaphor of God as Friend has been expanded by Sallie McFague in *Models of God* to consider God as Friend of the World. As friend to the world, "God has chosen to be in such a relationship with the world, to be bonded with it freely and in full commitment to its well being."[23] In light of this relationship, we are able more easily to understand that God's love and concern is not just for human life but for all life and for the life of the planet we inhabit. Rosemary Radford Ruether insists that even though humans have some rights to use other creatures, we are caught up in a "community of interdependence" that demands that we reverence and care for the rest of creation. "... There is an ultimate thouness at the heart of every other living being, whether it be a great mountain lion or swaying bacteria, that declares its otherness from us."[24] Creation and every creature in it are related to God and to one another. All of creation does not exist solely for the benefit of humanity. God loves this world, cares for it, sustains it. The implications for ecological reverence and nuclear responsibility are unavoidable. We humans now have the power once thought to be the province of God alone. We can determine whether or not life in its many forms will endure. We are challenged to be Godlike and care for and befriend Earth and all the life that it sustains.[25]

Whatever words we use to express our belief in God, "The point of all such theological constructs is to communicate certain basic truths about God: that it is of the essence of God to be in relationship; that there is no room for inequality or hierarchy in

God; that the personal reality of God is the highest possible expression of love and freedom; that the mystery of divine life is characterized by self-giving and self-receiving; that divine life is dynamic and fecund, not static or barren."[26]

### Questions for Reflection

1. Make as long a list as possible of images and metaphors for God. Think of human and non-human metaphors. Which are you more comfortable with?

2. Who is the God you no longer believe in? Who is the God you now believe in?

3. What did you think God was like when you were seven or eight; when you were sixteen or seventeen? What do you think God is like now?

4. Write your own creed. I believe.... I believe....

5. Reflect on the consequences of believing that God is the Friend of the Earth. Does this metaphor appeal to you?

### Endnotes

1. Simone Weil, *Waiting for God* (New York: Harper & Row, 1973) 32.

2. Mary Daly, *Beyond God the Father: Toward a Philosophy of Women's Liberation* (Boston: Beacon Press, 1973) 28-31. See her "Autobiographical Preface to the 1975 Edition" of *The Church and the Second Sex* (Boston: Beacon Press, 1985) and *Gyn/ecology* (Boston: Beacon Press, 1978).

3. Catherine Mowry LaCugna, "The Relational God: Aquinas and Beyond," *Theological Studies* 46 (1985) 647.

4. See Catherine Mowry LaCugna, *God With Us: The Trinity and Christian Life* (New York: HarperCollins, 1991) and Elizabeth Johnson, *She Who Is: The Mystery of God in Feminist Theological Discourse* (New York: Crossroad, 1992). Also, Gail Ramshaw-Schmidt, "Naming the Trinity: Orthodoxy and Inclusivity" *Worship* 60:6 (November 1986).

5. Elizabeth Johnson, *She Who Is*, 150.

6. Ibid., 146.

7. LaCugna, *God With Us*, 210-211.

8. LaCugna, "The Relational God," 659.

9. Johnson, *She Who Is*, 227.

10. Ibid., 211.

11. Sandra Schneiders, *Women and the Word* (New York: Paulist Press, 1986).

12. Ibid., 23-24.

13. Ian Barbour, *Myths, Models and Paradigms* (New York: Harper &

Row, 1974) 161.

14. Mary Daly, *Beyond God the Father* (Boston: Beacon Press, 1973) 19.

15. Anne Carr, *Transforming Grace* (San Francisco: Harper & Row, 1988) 138-139.

16. Paul Tillich, *Dynamics of Faith* (New York: Harper & Row, 1957) 431.

17. Joanmarie Smith, "Lords, Kings and Warriors" in *PACE 15* (Winona, MN: St. Mary's Press, 1984-5).

18. Janet Morley, "In God's Image" *Cross Currents* 32:3 (Fall, 1982).

19. Ibid., 314.

20. Sallie McFague, *Models of God: Theology for an Ecological, Nuclear Age* (Philadelphia: Fortress Press, 1987) 179.

21. "Justice in the World" (Washington, D.C.: United States Catholic Conference, 1972) 34.

22. Sallie McFague, *Metaphorical Theology: Models of God in Religious Language* (Philadelphia: Fortress Press, 1982) and *Models of God: Theology for an Ecological, Nuclear Age* (Philadelphia: Fortress Press, 1987).

23. McFague, *Models*, 71.

24. Rosemary Radford Ruether, *Gaia and God: An Ecofeminist Theology of Earth Healing* (New York: HarperCollins, 1992) 227.

25. For a fuller description of the connection between the exploitation of Earth and the oppression of women, see Elizabeth Johnson, *Women, Earth and Creator Spirit* (New York: Paulist Press, 1993).

26. Catherine Mowry LaCugna, "The Baptismal Formula, Feminist Objections and Trinitarian Theology," *Journal of Ecumenical Studies*, 26:2 (Spring 1989) 246.

3

# $\mathcal{J}$esus the $\mathcal{C}$hrist

$\mathcal{I}$f you were to visit the boyhood home of President John F. Kennedy in Boston, you would find many of the relics of the Kennedy family intact—piano, crib, christening dress, and toys. As you moved from room to room, the recorded voice of Rose Kennedy, matriarch of that extraordinary family, would explain that this is the window seat where Jack sat on rainy days, the crib he slept in, the piano he practiced on, the christening dress he wore at his baptism, the toys he played with. It is as if the whole house were a memorial to him, as if it all existed primarily for him. Of course when he was growing up, that was not so. All of the brothers and sisters played on the piano, all slept in the crib, all were baptized in the same dress. But because of subsequent history, each of the items took on new meaning, new significance. We look back at his childhood through the lens of his presidency and tragic death. We do it all the time. When we think of a loved one who has died, we remember the good times and the bad through the filter of the loss. Subsequent events shape our memories.

The gospels operate in somewhat the same way. The disciples looked back at the years spent with Jesus through the lens of his tragic death and glorious resurrection. What they remembered

49

and told to one another, what they eventually wrote down were colored by the drama of the passion and resurrection. What we have in the gospels is not a transcript of what happened, not a biography of Jesus, but faith statements of the early community. When we read the gospels we are reading about what different communities thought of Jesus. Each of the gospels has a unique perspective, each contributes to the whole picture which we in the twentieth century construct. We are not only reading something about Jesus, something about the community that wrote about him, but also a great deal about the translations and interpretations this material has been assigned through the years.

Mary Rose D'Angelo maintains that two traumatic events colored the memories the early Christians had of Jesus: 1) the death and resurrection of Jesus and 2) the destruction of the temple in 70 CE. Their memories served to explain these dramatic events. "In attempting to speak of the Jesus of history, we in a sense try to redo what the gospels did—to bring Jesus into our present, to see him as his companions did and yet with our own twentieth-century eyes."[1]

It is the responsibility of each succeeding generation to discover for itself, with the benefit of the contributions of the past, what Jesus means for our day. What this suggests is that we are part of the tradition, we are traditioning, both receiving and contributing. We do not look to scripture for all the answers to today's questions. We endeavor, rather, to bring today's questions and today's answers into conversation with what we perceive to be biblical questions and answers. We bring together the past and the present in the light of the future reign of God. We neither canonize some past moment or our own present concerns, but rather we seek final answers in both.

Each age must respond to the revelation of God afforded it. Each age needs to learn to read the signs of the times. In reading the signs of the times, feminist theologies, like all liberation theologies, have a two-fold task: denouncing what is evil and announcing what is good. Denouncing, while critical to the process, is often the more problematic of the two. It involves looking at symbols, myths, beliefs, and customs that have oppressed, even as they were held dear.

Christology has proven to be the most difficult area to critique because some people think that questioning how the symbol of Jesus has been used against women is to deny the very being and message of Jesus. I do not believe this is so, and I will therefore consider the negative aspects of Christology as regards women and then the positive impact as understood from a feminist perspective.

### Christology's Negative Impact

Part of that work of denouncing/announcing is being carried out by feminist theologians who repeatedly ask and are asked, "Can a male savior save women?" For some, notably Mary Daly, the answer is no. In spite of that "no" and of her identifying herself as Post-Christian, Daly's contribution in raising significant issues for feminist theologians cannot be discounted. She saw the oppression of women by church structures and practices, and she heard the questions before most others; she articulated them in a courageous and lucid manner. Issues she raised twenty years ago are still being struggled with. One of her concerns was what she called "Christolatry" and the effect the image of Jesus has had on women. Dorothee Söelle, German theologian, has labeled it Christofascism. Sadly, Christology is the Christian symbol that has most effectively marginalized women.

### Christology and Suffering

Daly's perception of Jesus as suffering servant, scapegoat for our sins, is a good illustration of the multivalenced quality of symbols. Symbols may take on different significances and meanings at different times in history. According to Daly, the sacrificial lamb, both in the Jewish tradition of Yom Kippur and of Jesus in his passion and death, have functioned to idealize the virtues of a victim: self-sacrificing love, humility, obedience, passivity, and acceptance of suffering as the will of God.[2]

She acknowledges that the symbol of Jesus as scapegoat may have inspired some women and men to holiness, but she sees its overall consequence as evoking intolerance for weak and marginal peoples among dominant and powerful people. Guilty at not living up to the model of Jesus as scapegoat for the sins of humankind and unable to accept one's own evil, the majority of powerful persons projected that guilt on to people in marginal positions. Women have been included on the margin in a dramatic way, having been defined in connection with sin and evil in the classic reading of the creation myth. As a result, they have been innocent victims and have been robbed even of the credit for their sacrifice.

A dramatic example of idealizing suffering as virtue is explored by Ann Loades, theologian from the British Isles, in the life of Simone Weil.[3] Weil's self-imposed victimhood resulted from destructive over-identification with the suffering Christ. In her essay on the French mystic who starved to death during the Second World War, Loades questions whether Weil should be revered for inflicting on herself the kind of death that so many others were forced to undergo in concentration camps. Loades maintains that what precipitated Weil's premature death was a theology that fostered a morbid over-identification with the suffering Christ.

Women, unable to act *in persona Christi* by reason of church laws, realize that they can imitate Christ "all too successfully if the Christ they imitate is the dead or dying Christ, rather than the Christ of the resurrection."[4] The destructive elements of Weil's theology are also evidenced in a prayer she composed shortly before her death. "That I may be unable to will any bodily movement, or even any attempt at movement, like a total paralytic. That I may be incapable of receiving any sensation, like someone who is completely blind, deaf, and deprived of all the senses. That I may be unable to make the slightest connection between two thoughts..."[5] Weil was a brilliant philosopher whose spiritual writings have nourished many. Her generosity, her courage, and her insightful mind might have survived to make an even greater contribution had she had another metaphor by which to live.

While not denying the destructive elements of a misguided devotion to the passion and sufferings of Jesus, it may be well before we leave this topic to recall that the image of the suffering Jesus has been healing and liberating for many. The music sung by Harriet Tubman, Sojourner Truth, and others like them who became liberators of their people, are clear examples of the power of bringing present experience and faith into dialogue. When slavery was seen through the lens of the sufferings of the exodus and of Jesus, decisive action was demanded, even of the frightened. Tubman, the "Moses" of her people, helped them to see their slavery through the metaphor of the crucified Christ. When she sang, they came to new understandings of their slavery and of what was now being demanded of them by Tubman and by God. Not only did they sing, "Nobody knows the trouble I see, Nobody knows like Jesus," they also sang, "Set my foot on de gospel ship and de ship begin to sail. It landed me on Canaan's shore, an' I'll never come back no mo'."[6] The journey to freedom, perilous as it was, was made possible because of the identification with the suffering Jesus.

When Sojourner Truth was asked if the source of her preaching was the bible, she replied "No, honey, can't preach from de Bible—can't read a letter. When I preaches, I has jest one text to preach from, an' I always preaches from this one. My text is 'When I found Jesus!'"[7] Christology in that case was redemptive, liberating. It redeemed the experience of slavery; it did not glorify suffering or gloss it over and deny it; it redeemed the experience of slavery and offered a challenge to journey toward the freedom of the sons and daughters of a loving God.

When speaking of the sufferings of women, it is important for well-fed, well-housed, well-educated women to remind themselves that their experience is not a universal one. It may be more accurate to speak of the varieties of women's experiences, using the plural for all three words. In her book *White Women's Christ and Black Women's Jesus*, which sets out that challenge, Jacqueline Grant presents a Black womanist view of Jesus who is regarded as Liberator in the light of Black women's triple oppression. "They share race suffering with Black men; with White women and other Third World women, they are victims of sexism; and with poor Blacks and Whites, and other Third World peoples, especially women, they are disproportionally poor."[8] Jesus identified with the least in society and he is a sign of hope in the struggle against oppression and for a liberated, resurrected existence. He is not a sign of romanticized contentment with oppression. His example tells us that it is not the acceptance of suffering but rather struggling against evil that is life-giving and holy.

In a powerful book, *Christianity, Patriarchy and Abuse*, the authors of the essays investigate the connection between violence and theological teachings that extol suffering and pain. They maintain that suffering *in itself* is not redemptive nor can it be redeemed. They question, for example, celebrating as salvific Christologies in which an angry Father demands the death of the perfect Son to save the rest of humanity, or Christologies in which the Father does not desire to punish but simply allows the son to suffer. The question is: Ought we tolerate such an image of God?

> To sanction the suffering and death of Jesus, even when calling it unjust, so that God can be active in the world only serves to perpetuate the acceptance of the very suffering against which one is struggling. The glorification of anyone's suffering allows the glorification of all suffering. To argue that salvation can only come through the cross is to make God a divine sadist and a divine child abuser.[9]

We must keep the cross and the resurrection as one. The cross is a sign of tragedy. "God's grief is revealed there and everywhere and every time life is thwarted by violence. God's grief is as ultimate as God's love. Every tragedy eternally remains and is eternally mourned. Eternally the murdered scream, 'Betrayal.' Eternally God sings kaddish [a mourner's prayer] for the world."[10]

### Christology and Anti-Semitism

For those who answer yes to the question whether a male savior can save women, the burden is still one of critiquing Christologies, judging what is constitutive to the life and teachings of Jesus and what is the destructive underbelly. In this process, feminists like Judith Plaskow have warned of a latent anti-Semitism which attributes all that is good to Jesus and all that is evil to the Jews, as if Jesus were not a Jew in life and in death.

The exaltation of Jesus by Christians has been a weapon against Jews and has enabled Christians to avoid responsibility for the excessive anti-Semitism of individual Christians and the church as a whole.

Feminists who are sensitive to the biases of the patriarchal paradigm need to be just as sensitive to the fact that we, too, carry with us our own biases regarding age, race, religion, class, and sex. The power of our culture is so overwhelming that we will be struggling with it till the end. Rosemary Radford Ruether maintains that "Theologically, anti-Judaism developed as the left hand of Christology. Anti-Judaism was the negative side of the Christian affirmation that Jesus was the Christ."[11]

Over the centuries, the Hebrew scriptures were held to be legalistic, concerned with the law and the letter of the law; the gospels, on the other hand were spoken of as the law of love. Christians reinterpreted the Hebrew scriptures in the light of the life, death, and resurrection of Jesus, as if they were all written, especially the prophets, in preparation for Jesus. The interpretations of the Jews were denied their own validity. Jews themselves were defined as victims of God's judgment for rejecting Jesus while Christians described themselves as the new chosen people of God. The church claimed to be the heir to the promise to Abraham, and the divine election of the Jews, to which God was so faithful, was denied. The prayers and rituals, especially the Holy Week liturgies with their prayers for "perfidious Jews," kept alive the flame of anti-Semitism.

In the light of pervasive Christian anti-Judaism, Susan Brooks Thistlethwaite calls herself a "recovering anti-Semite."[12] It is a reminder to all of us that we have been affected by the cultural and religious symbols, myths, and convictions of our past, and no matter how we try, we still carry around in us the residue of prejudice. The horror of the Holocaust has been the catalyst for Christian rethinking of this tragic history of hate. Dorothee Söelle, who lived during *Shoah* (the annihilation of the Holocaust), asks, "Is it possible that Christian training in obedience can be, even partially, responsible for the good conscience of a bureaucratic murderer?"[13]

## Christology and Maleness

We have only to recall the furor that erupted when Edwina Sandys' bronze sculpture, Christa, was hung a few years ago in the Episcopal Cathedral of St. John the Divine to understand the problem that the maleness of Jesus raises. Using the classic image of suffering, the crucifixion, Sandys presented a nude woman, broken and in agony. She was not proclaiming Jesus to be female but was uniting the sufferings of women to that of Christ. The image suggests that women have suffered in society and in the church unjustly, that their suffering is redemptive, and that women in their oppression image Christ. Her art forced people to think theologically and to question some long held beliefs. Christa was a statement about the reality of women's suffering and the inclusive nature of redemption. But it was a statement that caused conflict and resulted in accusations that such a portrayal demeaned Christ.

I have already mentioned the problem expressed in the question, "Can a male savior save women?" The basic issue is not whether Jesus was male or not; the issue is the way his maleness is being used theologically; the significance it is given. In the development of classical Christology, there was no interest in the maleness of Jesus. The traditional doctrine of the Incarnation speaks of the divinity and humanity of Jesus. The focus is on Jesus as Christ. "To put the matter simply, the Church, unlike the historian, the would-be portraitist, the biographer, or the psychiatrist, is not interested as such in Jesusology, but in Christology, in Jesus as the bearer of God's salvation."[14] The unfortunate use of the fact of Jesus' maleness (in the arguments against the ordination of women, for example), is virtually unprecedented. The exploitation of maleness as an essential element of Jesus' being as Christ is an effort to maintain the *status quo*.

The controversy regarding maleness came to the fore in the discussions on the ordination of women. The argument developed thus: If the celebrant of Eucharist represents and images a male Jesus, then the celebrant must be male. The Vatican declaration, "Women in the Ministerial Priesthood" uses Thomas Aquinas's argument that sacramental signs represent what they signify by natural resemblance. Because Thomas's under-standing of women was "being in subjection," it followed that he opposed ordaining women since one born in a state of subjection could not "signify any superiority of rank."

The document refers to the natural resemblance that must oc-cur between Christ and the presider at Eucharist and states that "When Christ's role in the Eucharist is to be expressed sacra-mentally, there would not be this 'natural resemblance' which must exist between Christ and his minister if the role were not taken by a man: in such a case it would be difficult to see in the minister the image of Christ. For Christ himself was and remains a man."[15] The statement borders on heresy. We might ask if the authors' understanding of women is that of "being in sub-jection." We might ask how the writers interpret Galatians 3:27-28. If in Baptism into Christ, we have all put on Christ and are all one in Christ, how did women get excluded from this re-lationship?

### Reclaiming Jesus the Christ

Jesus has been called a feminist,[16] but I do not believe that is a title he deserves. While each age reinterprets the bible according to its own lights, it is anachronistic to read modern issues, un-known two thousand years ago, back into the first century. The best we can do is examine to see if the values and concerns of Jesus and the values and concerns of feminists are consistent with one another or if they are so diametrically opposed that one or the other must be abandoned. The study of the gospels is not for the purpose of discovering in Jesus a model to imitate. Daly questioned the role that models have had on people and insists that true leaders tend to encourage others to shuck off imitation and discover their own unique being. "Jesus or any other liber-ated person who has this effect functions as a model precisely in the sense of being a model-breaker, pointing beyond his or her own limitations to the potential for further liberation."[17]

Much of what we believe about Jesus is constructed from his teachings, his parables, and from the kind of community that formed around him. Some women, bringing their own life ex-perience into conversation with those teachings, parables, and community have recognized community, liberation, and peace as significant Christological subjects.

Kenyan theologian Teresa M. Hinga, after decrying the imperial images of Christ that accompanied colonialism, suggests that when Africans began to appropriate images of Christ enshrined in the New Testament, they were able to throw off the distortions of colonial praxis and claim Christ the Liberator. "For Christ to become meaningful in the context of women's search for emancipation, he would need to be a concrete and personal figure who engenders hope in the oppressed by taking their [women's] side, to give them confidence and courage to persevere."[18] Moreover, Christ would enable them to speak for themselves. The image of Christ that Hinga describes relates not merely to the personal, but is also concerned with the lot of victims of social injustice and the dismantling of unjust social structures.

### Community of Equals[19]

Ironically, when most theology was being developed by celibate males, family was a dominant metaphor for the church. As married women and men develop theology, that image is not so central. As a matter of fact, it is, in some cases, rejected. Elisabeth Schüssler Fiorenza describes the community around Jesus as a discipleship of equals where the model of the patriarchal family was eliminated. Over and over, Jesus taught that domination was not the pattern for relationships among his followers. He included marginal people among his disciples: the poor, the outcast, and sinners. It was a community where the first would be counted last and where whoever would be great among the disciples must be servant to the others. It was a community in which Jesus washed the feet of his friends and commanded them to do the same.

"Whoever does not receive the kingdom of God like a child shall not enter it" (Mk 10:15). Our modern romantic notions concerning childhood were not what was operating here. At that time, children and slaves were among the "least" in the patriarchal family. So often misunderstood as a call to a childlike attitude toward life, this saying is rather a challenge not to dominate others. The presence of children mentioned by all three synoptic writers leads us to conclude that the community that Jesus gathered made a place for children and cared for them. Jesus' statements about children are consistent with the repeated injunctions not to seek to be first but be last and servant of all (Mk 9:35); not to imitate those who lord it over others (Mk 10:42), but to appreciate that Jesus was among them as one who serves (Lk 22:27).

While children are specifically included in the community, patriarchal fatherhood is specifically excluded. Mark records that whoever does the will of God is mother, brother, and sister to Jesus. Fathers are listed among those things that are left behind: "Truly, I say to you, there is no one who has left house or brothers or sisters or mother or father or children or lands for my sake and for the gospel, who will not receive a hundredfold now in this time," but they are not among the hundredfold promised: "houses, and brothers and sisters and mothers and children and lands..." (Mk 10:29-30). Fiorenza interprets this to mean, not a rejection of fathers as we know them, but a rejection of the patriarchal father who could dominate his extended family. Most men were not patriarchs but were under the law of patriarchy. Their lot was preferable to that of women, children, and slaves, but they were still among the subordinates.

Matthew enjoins the community to call no one father because "you have one Father, who is in heaven" (23:9). The realization of the fatherhood of God is a renunciation of the power, prestige, and authority of patriarchy. The sisters and brothers of the discipleship of equals were prohibited from exercising power over or against one another. Their confidence was in a loving God who was their father.

D'Angelo suggests that the discipleship of equals may have been a prophetic community where not just Jesus but many women and men prophesied, proclaimed the Reign of God, and effected cures and exorcisms. By way of example, she sets the woman who anointed Jesus in the tradition of Samuel and Nathan, who anointed Saul, David, and Solomon. She also presents Mary at Cana, the Samaritan woman, and Martha and Mary as instances of women acting without the commissioning or consent of Jesus. She suggests that we refer to the movement not as the Jesus movement but as the Reign-of-God movement since it is unlikely that either Jesus or his companions focused on his person during his lifetime. "By locating Jesus the prophet within a prophetic movement we envisage a situation in which Jesus participates in Sophia/Spirit in a prophecy shared with women and men of the movement... [who] emerge from disciple-ship to appear as Jesus' companions in the spirit."[20]

In our day, it is difficult to recognize many remnants of the discipleship of equals or of the Reign-of-God movement. At our best, we declare in our official documents, homilies, and lec-tures, that Paul was right. "For as many of you as were baptized into Christ have put on Christ. There is neither Jew nor Greek; there is neither slave nor free, there is neither male nor female; for you are all one in Christ" (Gal 3:27-28). But the theology we profess is not the theology by which we operate. We must con-fess that we are a church that discriminates in its practice against people of color, the poor, and women. It is not, as Hilaire Belloc said, that Christianity has failed. It has not been tried.

### Liberation

Feminist theology is a theology of liberation and as such it shares with the other liberation theologies the Christological ti-tle: Jesus Christ, Liberator. Elizabeth Johnson describes Jesus as Liberator, "not in a violent or military way, but through active ministry, boldness in speaking, steadfastness in conflict, suf-fering love, and ultimate reliance on God."[21] The very language she uses suggests how difficult liberation may be—"active, bold, steadfast, suffering." While not denying ultimate reliance upon God, we cannot allow that reliance to blind us to our own re-sponsibility in the process. We are not talking here about vi-olence or militarism but neither are we talking about a passive reliance that God alone will come through and free us. Liberation is never a pure gift, much as it comes to us from God. Liberation is a journey that requires of us action, boldness, stead-fastness, and suffering as we participate with God in the elimina-tion of sin in its many forms.

Freedom and liberation have been romanticized; they are

sometimes misinterpreted as one-time events when all shackles are broken and all is sweetness and light. Not so. Liberation is a process in which two difficult conversions are accomplished concurrently: conscientization[22] and the transformation of society. Conscientization is that process whereby persons gain some depth in interpreting their problems, are conscious of the biases (their own and those of others) that are operating, and assume responsibility for their lives. While we speak of personal and societal transformation as two, they are one; as people change the way they think, society is changed, and as society changes, patterns of thinking are also altered. Liberation is hard work. God did not carry the Israelites magically from slavery to the promised land. They struggled forty years in the desert as they moved toward liberation.

When we speak of Jesus Christ as liberator, we mean that in his life and teaching Jesus was on the side of marginal people. He was concerned with liberating people from their poverty, their suffering, and their sin. When he returned to Nazareth and announced his mission, he chose to read from Isaiah in the synagogue: "The Spirit of the Lord is upon me, because he has anointed me to preach the good news to the poor. He has sent me to proclaim release to the captives and recovery of sight to the blind, to set at liberty those who are oppressed, to proclaim the acceptable year of the Lord" (Lk 4:18-19). His deeds and his behavior reinforced these words. His professed theology and his operative theology were congruent.

Trusting in his words, we are able to assume the difficult task of divesting ourselves of the myths that support oppressive situations and to risk overcoming that oppression. But the first step in the journey is to recognize systemic sin, the oppressive situations that prevent persons from becoming fully human. Often the oppression is so pervasive and long-lived that we are unable to see it. It appears to be "the way things are," and even the way they ought to be. Martin Luther King once said that one of his most difficult tasks was to help some Blacks to recognize their own oppression. Many of them saw that they were better off than previous generations, some owned homes and businesses, most were better educated than their parents. The security of small gains was seductive, and the effort required seemed too much to demand. Fear of freedom blinded them to the inequities that still existed. Fear made them incapable of accepting the consequences of bold, steadfast action. They sometimes chose the comfort of security rather than the risk of freedom.

Women also suffer from fear of freedom. The small economic, political, and social advances are too much to put into jeopardy by facing the pervasiveness of sexism in the church and society. They are, after all, better off than their mothers and grandmothers. They have the vote, they are better educated, better employed, they are ordained in some churches, and in others are even able to serve as lectors and extraordinary ministers of the Eucharist on some occasions! They have learned that life proceeds more easily when they are compliant. Rocking the boat threatens not only their position in society, but also their image of themselves as a good woman. Women have been and, unfortunately, still are being encultured to find their identity in pleasing others.

Jesus Christ, Liberator may not be the most consoling of titles, but it may be one that encourages us to assume responsibility for cooperating with the Spirit in the coming of the Reign of God. However, we must not let it lull us into a false security that God will take care of everything if only we pray and wait patiently. We are responsible. Liberation through Jesus Christ is a function of the Christian community. God acts in this world through human beings.

Ruether understands Liberator to have a close connection to the servanthood of which Jesus spoke. Neither slaves nor masters can serve as models for that kind of servanthood. "The essence of servanthood is that it is possible only for liberated persons, not people in servitude. Also it exercises power and leadership, but in a new way, not to reduce others to dependency, but to empower and liberate others."[23] Liberation is a call to action, to responsibility, to ministry. Liberation does not make following Christ easy. It may make it more demanding.

### Jesus as Peacemaker

When I was a child we did not speak of Jesus as peacemaker.

Instead, we sang: "An army of youth flying the banner of truth, we are fighting for Christ the King....For our flag, for our church, for Christ the King." At confirmation, I became a soldier of Christ and received a (gentle) slap in the face from the bishop, to remind me that I must be ready to suffer in the conflict against evil. In high school and college I studied the requirements for a just war. On the evening news I watched clergy bless bombs and tanks and guns. Sure that God was on our side, we did not hesitate to kill with those blessed bullets and bombs. The enemy probably also killed with their blessed bullets and bombs.

We have shifted from that position, in the light of the inhumanity of the Holocaust, Hiroshima, and Nagasaki. The unholy horror we unleashed on one another forced us to question what kind of a God could possibly sanction, much less sanctify, our behavior. Our history of holy wars, some of them recorded in scripture, of religious wars like the Crusades against the infidels, today's pseudo-religious wars of Christian against Christian, and Christian against Jew, and Christian against Muslim have forced us to reconsider our images of God and of Jesus. The warrior God, Yahweh Sabaoth, has not yet given way to the Prince of Peace, but the process has begun.

It is strange that we use so much peace language in reference to Jesus and that it took so long for us to take the words to heart. The celebration of his birth is accompanied by "Peace on earth to all of good will." We read his words, "Peace be to you...go in peace, your faith has cured you...my peace I leave you." We share a greeting of peace in our rituals. And yet, we are still not committed to peace. Once more our professed theology outstrips our operative theology. But there is cause for hope. Men and women who have taken the commitment to peace seriously have been writing, lecturing, demonstrating, praying, and suffering for the cause of peace.

Women have been stereotyped as more peace-loving, more compassionate, and more gentle than men. I do not believe that women are so by nature. If women have developed these characteristics, that is just what they are—developed characteristics. Women have learned to cultivate the more humane virtues while men have been encouraged to cultivate assertive, independent,

and competitive ones. This is a cultural phenomenon. To say this
is to suggest that it can be changed. Women and men can both
learn to be compassionate, independent, gentle, and assertive. A
feminist focus on Jesus as peacemaker is not the consequence of
an inherently placid nature.

Mary Elsbernd[24] presents two possible connections between
the gospel and pacifism which I believe may be applied more
broadly to the connection between the gospel and the pursuit of
peace. The first is a separatist understanding that interprets
Jesus' words as referring to a spiritual reality. Peace is not dependent on human effort, but rather it is a gift of God. The peace
referred to is interior, individual, and often leads to withdrawal
from the rest of society which is perceived as destructive of the
divine harmony. We see this lived out in the peace sects and
communities who stand apart from the culture and live by a radical and spiritual understanding of Jesus' words. A negative side
of this separatist perception is that the separatists tend to absent
themselves from any effort to construct peaceful institutions and
structures outside of the sect.

An alternative reading of the gospel regarding peace is based
on a belief in the Incarnation, which teaches that one of us is
God. Humanity, blessed in creation and called good by the
Creator, is now reconciled with the Divine in a unique fashion in
Jesus. The example of Jesus, who involved himself in the political, religious, and cultural concerns of his day, demands involvement not retreat. Moreover, the teaching of Jesus exacts an
active and dynamic response. Consider just two indications of
Jesus' commitment to peace: the beatitudes, and the injunction to
love our enemies.

Luke lists only four beatitudes: "Blessed are you poor, for
yours is the kingdom of God. Blessed are you that hunger now
for you shall be satisfied. Blessed are you that weep now, for you
shall laugh. Blessed are you when others hate you, and when
they exclude you and revile you and cast out your name as evil,
on account of the Son of man" (Lk 6:20-22). Matthew, on the other hand, has expanded (and somewhat spiritualized) them to
eight: Blessed are the poor in spirit, those who mourn, the meek,
those who hunger for righteousness, the merciful, the single

hearted, the peacemakers, and those who are persecuted for righteousness sake (Mt 5:3-12). It is as if these beatitudes build to a crescendo. Peacemaking is the culmination, not possible without the others. If we were asked to list these characteristics of those who would be peacemakers, we would probably include avoiding an attitude of acquisitiveness that leads to buying, consuming, saving, squandering, wasting; the ability to mourn the loss or breaking up of a relationship; the tolerance, forbearance, and gentility of meekness; the commitment to righteousness, justice, and mercy; avoiding deception, fraud, and duplicity, and remaining single hearted. But we cannot stop there. The next beatitude warns that persecution will follow a commitment to the struggle for justice or righteousness.

The command to love our enemies has been called Jesus' most scandalous teaching.[25] A scandal is something that gets in the way, an obstacle. The love of neighbor as ourselves is not a scandal, but the love of the enemy is; it is a stumbling block. Christians are enjoined to love our enemies, do good to those who hate us, bless those who curse us, and pray for those who abuse us (Lk 6:27-28). Such peacemaking endeavors require deep conversion. Peace is not an abstract or theoretical principle but one that must be lived out in the here and now. Peace-making is not tolerating the intolerable. It is effected by participating in the transformation of the world.

Jesus as peacemaker is a deceiving image. It has produced a sentimental and romantic notion of peace. Like liberation, peace is hard work. It is not a warm fuzzy feeling. It is not merely a cessation of conflict or the absence of strife. Peace sometimes exists in the midst of confrontation and active resistance to evil. The American Catholic bishops when speaking of Jesus in the Peace Pastoral use the words courage, conversion, justice, forgiveness, and reconciliation. The pursuit of peace requires courage because the hard lesson about peace is that there is no peace without justice.

The absence of overt conflict and violence does not equal peace. Oppression of any kind is in itself violence. It is the first level of violence. The second level occurs when oppressed people confront that violence; it is usually at this point that the popular culture accuses oppressed people of violence, and it responds with violence. But the spiral began in the unjust situation of oppression. American Blacks in the civil rights movement were accused of violence. Women who confront abuse in a marriage by leaving or bringing charges against an abusive husband are accused of violating the family. In the past numerous women were encouraged to remain in an abusive relationship because it was "God's will" or because of the sacramentality of marriage. Living in such a situation is not living in peace.

### What Feminists Are Not Addressing

You may have noticed that feminist theologians are not especially focusing on the classical doctrines about Jesus the Christ. The doctrines concerning Jesus that were defined in the first few centuries of the church's life resulted from questions raised in the context of the lives of the early Christians. Today our questions are arising out of our own context. When the Jewish Christians thought about Jesus, they used and reinterpreted in Jewish categories. Jews knew God from the action of God in the life of the Israelites. God saved, protected, liberated. Jesus was understood in the light of the Jewish scriptures. As early Christians read the bible, they recognized Jesus as Messiah, as Sophia, the Wisdom of God, and as Suffering Servant. Each of the evangelists wrote from a different perspective and provided the early church with a variety of Christologies.

As the church expanded and included more and more non-Jews, Greek categories of thinking affected the articulation of Christology. How explain Jesus' divinity; how explain the relationship between his divinity and his humanity? One side of the argument denied the divinity of Jesus. Arius, for example, taught that Jesus was above all other creatures but questioned his divinity since God could not be limited or finite. The Council of Nicea in 325 proclaimed that Jesus is the only begotten Son of the Father, not a creature made by the Father. He is not a super-creature but partakes in the divine life and substance.

At the other end of the spectrum, there were those who questioned the humanity of Jesus. The teachings of Apollinaris, who emphasized the divinity of Jesus and said that Jesus had no human soul at all, was condemned at the first Council of Constantinople in 381. Nestorius, condemned at the Council of Ephesus in 431, believed that the Word of God became human (giving up divinity, as it were) in the Incarnation and that such ideas as Mary being the Mother of God or God suffering made no sense.

The divinity or the humanity of Jesus are not the significant questions for most theologians today. Their question, and ours, is what do the teachings, life, death, and resurrection of Jesus have to say to the twentieth century and beyond?

### Questions for Reflection

1. Recall some of the more famous portrayals of Jesus in art. Then recall some of the scriptural images of Jesus. In what ways are they different?

2. How can we reconcile the image of a gentle loving Jesus with that of Jesus the Liberator?

3. How would you answer the challenge that because Jesus was male, males hold a different position in the scheme of salvation?

4. In what ways might we Christians overcome the anti-Semitism inherent in some Christologies?

5. What do you think the teachings of Jesus have to say to the twentieth century and beyond?

### Endnotes

1. Mary Rose D'Angelo, "Re-membering Jesus: Women, Prophecy and Resistance in the Memory of the Early Churches," *Horizons* 19:2 (1992) 204.

2. Mary Daly, *Beyond God the Father* (Boston: Beacon Press, 1973) 75-77.

3. Ann Loades, *Searching for Lost Coins*, Princeton Theological Monograph Series (Allison Park, PA: Pickwick Publications, 1987) 39-60.

4. Ibid., 43.

5. Quoted by Loades, 48.

6. In John Lovell, Jr., *Black Song* (New York: Macmillan, 1972).

7. Quoted by Jacquelyn Grant in *White Women's Christ and Black Women's Jesus: Feminist Critique and Womanist Response* (Atlanta: Scholars Press, 1989) 214.

8. Ibid., 216.

9. Joanne Carlson Brown and Rebecca Parker, "For God So Loved the World?" in *Christianity, Patriarchy and Abuse* edited by Joanne Carlson Brown and Carole R. Bohn (New York: Pilgrim Press, 1989) 23.

10. Ibid., 27.

11. Rosemary Radford Ruether, *To Change the World: Christology and Cultural Criticism* (New York: Crossroad, 1981) 31.

12. Susan Brooks Thistlethwaite, *Sex, Race and God: Christian Feminism in Black and White* (New York: Crossroad, 1989) 95.

13. Dorothee Söelle, *Beyond Mere Obedience* (New York: Pilgrim Press, 1982) 9.

14. R.A. Morris, Jr., "The Ordination of Women and the Maleness of Christ," *Anglican Theological Review*, Supplementary Series, 6 (June, 1976) 72.

15. Sacred Congregation for the Doctrine of the Faith, "Declaration on the Admission of Women to the Ministerial Priesthood." *Origins* 6:33 (February 3, 1977).

16. See Leonard Swidler, "Jesus Was a Feminist," *The Catholic World*, January 1971, 177-183.

17. Daly, *Beyond God*, 75.

18. Teresa M. Hinga, "Jesus Christ and the Liberation of Women" in *The Will to Arise: Women, Tradition and the Church in Africa* edited by Mercy Amba Oduyoye and Musimbe R.A. Kanyoro (Maryknoll: Orbis Books, 1992) 191-2.

19. For a fuller discussion of the discipleship of equals, see Elisabeth Schüssler Fiorenza, *In Memory of Her: A Feminist Theological Reconstruction of Christian Origins* (New York: Crossroad, 1983) 140-151.

20. D'Angelo, "Re-membering Jesus," 207-208.

21. Elizabeth A. Johnson, *Consider Jesus: Waves of Renewal in Christology* (New York: Crossroad, 1990) 93.

22. Philosopher of education Paulo Freire discusses the process of con-scientization or the developing of a critical consciousness in his classic work, *Pedagogy of the Oppressed* (New York: Herder and Herder, 1971).

23. Ruether, *To Change the World*, 54.

24. Mary Elsbernd, *A Theology of Peacemaking: A Vision, a Road, a Task.* (Lanham, MD: University Press of America, 1989) 102-106.

25. Donald Senior, C.P. "Jesus' Most Scandalous Teaching" in *Biblical and Theological Reflections on 'The Challenge of Peace'* edited by John Pawlikowski, O.S.M. and Donald Senior, C.P. (Wilmington, DE: Michael Glazier, 1984) 55-72.

# 4

# What It Means to Be Human

One of the most significant theological questions turns on the issue of what it means to be human. Philosophers and more recently anthropologists, psychologists, and sociologists have studied humans to discover what makes them different from other animals and what they hold in common. Some characteristics that have been suggested are: the ability to assign meaning to phenomena, to symbolize; awareness of death; awareness of the future that enables us to plan ahead, and finally, the ability to blush. Mark Twain, in noting that only humans blush, remarked that only humans have reason to blush. It is widely agreed that while humans hold some things universally, human nature is not some fixed entity, but rather is affected by the culture in which people exist.

## Male and Female; Masculine and Feminine

The French say it well, "Vive la difference!" Women and men are obviously different; their sex organs are different, as is their hormonal structure. The question is, do these differences constitute a difference *in nature?* Or are the differences only bio-logical and therefore not a firm basis for a theory that holds that women and men have different natures? Have differences in sex determined the differences we assign to gender?

Gender and sex are frequently misused words; they are used as if they refer to the same thing. They do not. Sex has to do with bodies that are either male or female. Maleness and femaleness are determined before birth; they are physiological givens. But we are more alike than we are different. Women and men have 46 chromosomes; only one determines femaleness or maleness.

On the other hand, masculinity and femininity are gender cat-egories that are culturally assigned designations and often change in different times and places. What is considered fem-inine in one culture might be perceived as masculine in another. Americans traveling in some countries abroad are surprised to see men walking hand-in-hand or with their arms around one another's shoulders. Such behavior, according to the American culture, is feminine; in other climes, it is masculine.

Dual-nature anthropology suggests that women and men are of different natures determined by God and that these different natures determine what is appropriate for each sex. We will ex-amine this attitude. I will also look into some aspects of the sin-gle-nature theory that holds that most differences between women and men are culturally defined and therefore open to change. Finally I will consider an anthropology-in-the-making that suggests that we do not yet know what it means to be hu-man as males or females.

### Two-Nature Anthropology

While it has never been explicitly stated in official church doc-uments, a dualism inherited from the Greeks has influenced much of the theology developed through the ages. Traditional categories include such dualisms as form/matter, soul/body, spiritual/material, God/Israel, Christ/Church, male/female. These dualities lead to a kind of thinking that sets the partners in each pair at odds with one another by defining them as op-posites. The first of each pair is determined to be the better; the second is somewhat lesser, dependent upon, and derivative from the first. Israel depends upon God in a way that God does not depend upon Israel; the church depends upon Christ in a way that Christ does not depend upon the church. And so it is with the soul and the body and with women and men.

The Greeks thought that spiritual reality was unitary; duality only appeared with matter. Therefore God, being spirit, can not be dual nor can the spiritual part of human beings be dual. The spiritual must be unitary; bodiliness causes duality. Bodiliness, with its attendant feelings, emotions, and desires, is lesser and suspect. Because of women's "bodiliness"—menstruation, lactation, and the ability to give birth—they were more easily associated with the bodily and men were associated with the spiritual side of humanity. The association of femaleness with bodiliness caused women to be perceived as less rational, less intelligent, less able for rigorous thought, less responsible for developing their minds. What was important was a woman's uterus.

At the beginning of the twentieth century, when women began to seek college degrees, rabid arguments were made against their higher education because it was thought that exercising their minds would do harm to their reproductive abilities. Martha Carey Thomas, president of Bryn Mawr, admitted to being terrified as a young woman after reading a popular essay by G. Stanley Hall. He concluded that college was fine for the training of those who do not marry. His warning that college may "perhaps come to be training stations of a new-old type, the agamic or agenic [i.e., sterile] woman, be she aunt, maid (old or young), nun, school teacher, or bachelor woman" left Thomas fearful that she would be a "pathological invalid" as a result of her education. She survived and thrived because of her education, but others were not so fortunate. Antoinette Brown, the first woman ordained in the United States, gave up the ministry after being convinced by the "scientific" argument.[1]

Dualistic thinking also had an impact on theology in spite of official statements as early as the Second Council of Constantinople (553 CE). This council condemned the teaching that the body was a degrading place to which the preexisting soul was consigned. In spite of this condemnation, a belief emerged that the image of God resides only in the spiritual part of humanity; that our bodies are not included in that definition. Gregory of Nyssa wrote that the original creation was monistic, spiritual, and that bodily nature, foreign to God, was added later.

The catechism used in many Catholic schools in years past illustrates this point well. Chapter one asks "What is man?" "Man," we are told, "is a creature composed of body and soul and made in the image and likeness of God." The follow-up question asks, "Is this likeness in the body or the soul?" And the answer is, "This likeness is chiefly in the soul." Even though the word "chiefly" somewhat qualifies the answer, the series of questions that follows focus on how the soul is like God. There are no questions about how the body may be in the image and likeness of God.[2]

The catechism questions are a shorthand way of explaining an attitude toward the body, and also toward women, which was held for centuries. Augustine explained it thus: "Woman together with her husband is in the image of God so that the whole substance may be one image; but when she is referred to separately in her quality of helpmate, which regards women alone, then she is not in the image of God. But as regards man alone, he is the image of God as fully and completely as when woman is joined to him in one."[3]

Centuries later, Thomas Aquinas made a distinction between the subordination of women and that of slaves. Thomas thought that slavery was not of the order of creation but was the result of sin and only to be tolerated because it was necessary for the maintenance of the social order. The male/female hierarchy, on the other hand, was of the order of creation. As he understood it, women were:

defective and misbegotten males...for the active power in the male seed tends to the production of a perfect likeness according to the male sex while the production of woman comes from a defect in the active power, or from some external influence, such as the south wind, which is moist, as the philosopher [Aristotle] observes.[4]

Few statements better exemplify the close connection between the knowledge available in each culture and the theology that is developed in that culture. The science of Aquinas's time taught that the male seed contained the whole new person. The seed, complete in itself, was deposited in the mother's womb much as a seed is placed in the ground to be nourished. Apple seeds produced apples, orange seeds produced oranges. If the seed did not produce according to its kind (in this case, a male), then there must have been something faulty with it or some external circumstance must have intervened.

The idea of women as defective males encouraged an attitude that contributed to the slaughter of women who were believed to be witches in the fifteenth, sixteenth, and seventeenth centuries. Two Dominicans, Heinrich Kramer and James Sprenger, commissioned by the Pope to codify the regulations regarding witchcraft, wrote: "All witchcraft comes from carnal lust which is in women insatiable."[5] And "as regards intellect, or the understanding of spiritual things, [women] seem to be of a different nature from men; a fact which is vouched for by the logic of authorities, backed by various examples from the scriptures."[6] Kramer and Sprenger also believed that the word "femina" was derived from "fe" and "minus" since women were weaker in holding to the faith. Perhaps they had not read of Mary Magdalen and the other women who remained with Jesus at the cross.

You might think that all of this has changed; no one seriously thinks that women and men are created by God with different natures. Not so. This thinking still influences some of our theology. As recently as 1976, the "Vatican Declaration on the Admission of Women to the Ministerial Priesthood" stated:

"Sacramental signs," says St. Thomas, "represent what they signify by natural resemblance." The same natural resemblance is required for persons as for things. When Christ's role in the Eucharist is to be expressed sacramentally there would not be this "natural resemblance" which must exist if the role of Christ were not taken by a man; in such a case it would be difficult to see in the min-

ister the image of Christ. For Christ himself was and remains a man.[7]

The circumlocution "not taken by a man" is an attempt to avoid
stating directly that if the role of Christ were taken by a woman,
it would be difficult to see in her the image of Christ. The point
has been made that one's anthropology, what one believes about
what it means to be human, has a dramatic effect on the theology
that is espoused. A 1979 papal address provides a hint of the anthropology out of which Pope John Paul II operates. When he
spoke to the Tenth National Congress of Italian Domestic
Workers he was addressing those women who clean other people's houses and the tourist hotels. He encouraged them to understand that "domestic work must be seen not as an implacable
and inexorable imposition, as slavery, but as a free choice, conscious and willing." The Pope then continued: "[Domestic work]
fully realizes women's nature and fulfills their needs."[8] It is difficult indeed to understand how the Pope could think that domestic work is what fulfills a woman!

The papal document "On the Dignity and Vocation of
Women" still speaks as though women are of a different nature
than men. True, it is acknowledged that women are fully human,
but the emphasis is on the complementary nature of the relationship between women and men. Women complete what is
wanting in men; therefore there are expectations and roles that
are appropriate for each, and there are others that are inappropriate. Not only does the document "focus our attention
on virginity and motherhood as two particular dimensions of the
fulfillment of the female personality" [#17], it maintains that
when Christ instituted the Eucharist, "it is legitimate to conclude
that he thereby wished to express the relationship between man
and woman, between what is "feminine" and what is "masculine" [#26]. The argument is then made for the necessity of the
celebrant to be male in order to maintain the symbolic "bridegroom and bride" relationship between the priest and the congregation.

An article on the teaching of Pope John Paul II by Sara Butler
discusses complementarity as an appropriate expression of the

"equal but different" ways of being woman or man. Moreover, she suggests that "Masculinity and femininity, two 'incarnations' of humanity, cannot be regarded as the product of culture. Nor are masculinity and femininity defined in terms of personality traits or psychological characteristics.... Femininity and masculinity have a specific 'original' meaning that is engraved in our bodies."[9]

It would be a mistake to think that Christian history has a monopoly on this anthropological dualism. In the Jewish tradition (changed only recently by some Jewish congregations), women may not be counted in the *minyan*, that body of ten men who must be present before prayer may begin. Ten males, even including a child, a drunk, or a mentally unbalanced male, would count, but not a holy woman. Some Jews still pray each morning, "Blessed art Thou, the Eternal, our God, King of the universe who hath not made me a woman."

We find traces of dualistic thinking in Islam also. The Laws of Manu teach that "In childhood, a female must be subject to her father, in youth to her husband. When her Lord, the husband is dead, to her sons; a woman must never be independent."[10]

Catherina Halkes maintains that the dualistic model works in two ways. In the first case, women are perceived to be lesser as man's helpmate, and therefore rightly set in a position to serve and to be protected from the evils of the world. In the second, they are seen as complementary to men, providing the feminine dimension of which men are incapable. Women can, or so the story goes, bring to the public sphere the nurturing and generative qualities displayed in the home. Women who act otherwise are suspect. The dualistic model denies that women may be able to function in the world in roles traditionally held by men.[11] The complementarity model ignores the witness of history and of experience; women and men are not entirely restricted to certain talents, abilities, and behaviors.

In its romantic form, the two-nature anthropology has led to both the subordination and the glorification of the "feminine." The mystique of the saintly mother, the good sister, the faithful wife, has cut women off from the public sphere and relegated them to the private sphere of the home where they create a haven for men who must work in the heartless world. Women have become the moral guardians of the home, the source of love and harmony. One has only to listen to TV or read the comic strips to discover another message; the exaltation of motherhood is belied by the plethora of mother and mother-in-law jokes. We might also question the image of the saintly mother as we consider the number of adults who are revealing the violence of their childhoods with mothers who were also batterers.

### Limits of Dual-Nature Anthropology

Dual-nature anthropology has been criticized on many counts. We will discuss four of them here: 1) it is "past" oriented; 2) it led to a spirituality that did not take the body into account sufficiently; 3) it fostered an asceticism that denied the dignity of the body; and 4) it defined women by their physiology.

When critiquing the dualistic model in its traditional manifestations we discover that it is "past" oriented. It defines women and men according to norms determined by life-styles and demands of another age. It does not take into account the questions, insights, and wisdom of the present age. It teaches that the revelation, traditions, customs, and morals of other ages have been determined by the Divine will and therefore may not be altered. Dualistic thinking strives to maintain the *status quo* as the natural order fixed by creation—as if what exists is from on high.

Dualistic anthropology has led to an easy acceptance of patriarchy, the rule of powerful men over less powerful men and women, as natural, as the way the world should be, as ordained by God. The cultural roles assigned to women and to men are seen as part of the divine plan from the beginning. Social and psychological attributes of each sex are deemed God-given and therefore unchangeable.

Two-nature anthropology also fostered the development of an ascetic spirituality that imaged the soul as being prisoner in the body and which spoke of death as the happy release of the soul from the enemy, the body. Some fathers and mothers of the desert, models of spirituality, fasted, used whips and chains to mortify their flesh, denied themselves sleep, and subjected their bodies to pain in every conceivable manner in order to free their souls for union with God. Such ascetic practices were an important facet of the life of monks, nuns, and laity alike. The purpose of this asceticism was the subjection of the body.

Dualistic thinking also contributed to a theology of sexuality that associated the body with animal nature and the soul with spiritual nature. Jerome, Augustine, and other early church fathers taught that intercourse, even between husbands and wives, was at least venially sinful. Fear and suspicion of all that was bodily produced a negative theology with which we are only recently beginning to come to grips. Modern scholarship has drawn a different picture of the relationship between soul and body and, as a result, a theology of sexuality is developing that honors the body as a gift from God, declared "good" at creation.

A final criticism of dualistic anthropology is that it tends to define women by their procreative abilities. "Anatomy is destiny" is the anthem: Woman's physiology determines her whole being. Every facet of her life is determined by her ability to bear children. Even women who are not mothers are defined in terms of motherhood. The 1988 document, "On the Dignity and Vocation of Women," speaks of virginity according to the gospel as "motherhood of the spirit." It calls on Romans 8:4 for validation: "So that the demands of the law might be fulfilled in us who live, not according to the flesh, but according to the spirit."[12] It is difficult to see the connection between being freed from the law of sin and death and spiritual motherhood. Women, we are told, are created to be mothers. No one says that men are created to be fathers.

### Feminist Dualism

Some find it surprising that there are also feminists who hold to a dual-nature anthropology, although the emphasis is different. They define evil as that which springs from maleness and patriarchy. They are separatists who seek in the community of women what has been denied them in the society of women and men. Perhaps the best known example is Mary Daly who writes that women are so alienated from their own being by patriarchy that only separatism allows for a release of a flow of Elemental Energy. "Thus understood, separatism is an essential aspect of gynophilic communication, for it separates a woman from the causes of fragmentation—the obstacles, internal and external—which separates her from the flow of integrity within her self."[13]

Separatism has been critiqued by other feminists such as Rosemary Radford Ruether as divisive not only between men and women but also divisive among women. Separatists have, on occasion, excluded from feminist gatherings women who have heterosexual relationships or who are mothers of male children or who still identify themselves as Christian or Jewish.[14]

In the feminist manifestation of a dual-nature anthropology, the patriarchal past is condemned. Ruether, however, proposes a more hopeful assessment, even as she acknowledges that all the inherited cultures today either ignore or sanction sexism. "All significant works of culture," she says, "have depth and power to the extent that they have been doing something else besides just sanctioning sexism."[15]

Rather than deny the past or condemn it as irreparably sexist, some women are searching for that hidden history which recognizes not only women's oppression but also women's contributions. These thinkers understand that women alone will not be able to create a new world, but that the cooperation of men and women is necessary in order to eliminate the dehumanizing aspects of our common history. They work toward creating social structures that will redeem both women and men in the belief that one can not be freed without the other. The system of patriarchy demeans women, but we must not lose sight of the fact that it also demeans men. The effects of patriarchy may be compared to the effect that slavery had on both slaves and masters. Slave-holders did not suffer in so dramatic and demeaning a way as the slaves, but the system of slavery held them in a different kind of bondage, restricting their ability to grow as full human beings.

The biblical support for a dualistic anthropology is rooted in the second recorded creation myth in which the woman is created as a helpmate for the man. In chapter seven, I will share some of the research of Phyllis Trible as she strives to reclaim that story from its misogynous applications.

### Single-Nature Anthropology

Biblical support for a one-nature anthropology begins in the first chapter of the book of Genesis. God created humanity in God's own image; in the image of God, male and female God created them. Simultaneously, God created them.

In the first chapter of the "Pastoral Constitution on the Church in the Modern World" the theologians of the Second Vatican Council interpret the creation myth to mean that persons are, by their inherent nature, created to be social beings who can not live or develop their potential outside of community. They remind us that when the Creator saw all that was created, it was very good. There is not the slightest suggestion that "image of God" is more applicable to males than to females.

Proponents of the single-nature model hold that to be a man or a woman is to be human or at least capable of growing toward the fully human. There is not a male way to be human and a female way to be human. There are no preordained roles or functions beyond the biological that are peculiar to men or to women. Women police officers, fire fighters and astronauts are proof that some women can do jobs better than some men. On the other hand, there are men who are more nurturing, more gentle, more generative than some women.

Personality and psychological traits have for the most part been described in oppositional categories. Assertiveness, independence, courage, and rationality are deemed masculine, while gentility, sentimentality, and generativity are assigned to women. Since there are courageous, gentle women and independent, sentimental men we would do better to describe human traits along a spectrum of qualities accessible to all, women and men alike. The restricting gender-assigned roles that culture has deemed appropriate to each sex have not been able to thwart the development of "inappropriate" characteristics in the opposite sex.

Modern research in sociology and psychology has brought us to the realization that much of what has been labeled masculine or feminine is culture-bound. The work of anthropologists like Margaret Mead taught us that what we believed to be "women's work" or "men's role" is not a universal experience.

There are tribes in which women and men play roles just opposite to those to which we are accustomed. Mead's classic study, *Sex and Temperament in Three Primitive Societies*,[16] revealed that one tribe, the Tchambuli, held to a reversal of the sex role stereotypes of our society. The men were gentle and nurturing and the women were aggressive. The second tribe, the Arapesh, were a people who were unaggressive, cooperative, and responsive to the needs of others, characteristics that our society has relegated to women. The third tribe, the Mundugumor, valued violent and aggressive behavior on the part of both females and males. Such cross-cultural data serve to disabuse us of some basic assumptions about what is nature.

Catherina Halkes suggests that one of the manifestations of the one-nature model may be called the emancipation model. This model is based on an abstract equality of the sexes. But as such, it may work negatively as well as positively.

> If the result is that only one sex is emancipated, that is, that the masculine norms remain the valid ones and women strive to reach them—then no real solution is offered. On the contrary, when the range of ways people can mature grows narrow, there is no openness to a critique of the one-sided masculine domination of our culture, and back comes the old patristic notion that a woman should become "as a man" (quasi vir).[17]

To believe that only women need emancipation implies that men are already freed. The objective then becomes for women to become as much like men as possible. If there is only one nature, and men are presumed to have had a better chance to develop humanly, then the best thing for women is to get a piece of the pie men have been enjoying for so long. Learn the tricks of surviving in the male system; beat them at their own game. The presumption that the male human has developed in a way that is more truly human than the female, is a dangerous one. It denies the worth of women's experience and history. It makes the male the norm for the human.

A discussion of single-nature anthropology would be incomplete without mention of androgyny. Androgyny, according to the *Oxford English Dictionary,* is "the union of sexes in one individual; hermaphroditism." In popular usage it means an individual who displays qualities and traits deemed appropriate in our society to both sexes. Androgynous persons are neither excessively masculine nor feminine in their personality. They possess a diversity based not on sex-typed roles but on individual and personal differences.

The androgynous model suggests that males and females possess capacities that are both masculine and feminine. This may be a good time to remember that the distinction between maleness and femaleness is a given, assigned long before birth, but that masculinity and femininity are cultural assignments. But the very use of the terms masculine and feminine serves to perpetuate the myth that there are attributes that may be properly designated as referring to men or to women. It may be better for us to begin to speak of human characteristics having "agentic" and "communal" attributes.

We act agentically when we are self-assertive; we act communally when we are building relationships. Using words like agentic and communal, instead of masculine and feminine, encourages the recognition that we are speaking of human personality characteristics common to both women and men. It also sets the discussion in the broader context of the community rather than in the more individual one of personal characteristics. Changing the language takes the emphasis off gender assignments and puts it rather on other aspects of human activity. If we used these or other non-gendered terms, women who are ambitious, initiating, and assertive would no longer be perceived as overly masculine and lacking in femininity. Nor would men who are gentle, relational, and aesthetic feel that they must make up for these qualities by adopting a macho attitude. Women and men alike might be able to perceive themselves as human beings who sometimes act independently as agents and who sometimes act communally.

### Limits of One-Nature Anthropology
One-nature anthropology neglects to take into consideration human bodiliness and hormonal differences. Some of the un-

answered questions are: How does a female body provide a different contact with the rest of reality than a male body? What effect do the experiences of menses, pregnancy, lactation, and menopause have on women? What effect on men who are deprived of these experiences? Why don't we speak more of men being deprived of the wonder that is the female body?

We have already discussed another problem to which one-nature anthropology can lead. If we take as the norm the way that men have been allowed to develop in our society, then women are still conceived as "deficient males" who must emulate male conduct in order to become fully human. Only in this way will women be able to be assimilated into personhood.

Another caution needs to be considered. In both the dual-nature and the unitary-nature models there is a danger that is so subtle that it is probably the greatest problem with both systems. The fact is that we do not yet know what woman is or what she may be. What we have in both cases is a male-defined female. Stymied by a patriarchal mind-set, we have not been courageous enough to imagine a truly different kind of woman (and man).

### Transformative Personal[18] Anthropology

Both of the preceding models are inadequate since they reflect society as it was (and unfortunately as it is), but not as it ought to be. Mary Buckley draws an explicit and close connection between human nature and the cultural structures that enable and support that nature. When the systems operative in a culture are demeaning and dehumanizing, a vicious circle is set in motion in which women and men are prevented from developing the full humanity to which they are called. At the same time, fractured humanity is incapable of creating a society that is truly human. It is impossible to change one without changing the other. We create and are created by the society in which we live. A new nature and the new society are possible only through conversion, metanoia; conversion not only of the individual but conversion of the oppressive structures of society. The two conversions must occur simultaneously. And as with all conversions, we are not able to foresee what will be.

Like the single-nature model, the transformative personal

model grows out of an awareness that culture and history have been created by people. But Buckley makes specific what is only hinted at in the one-nature theory. We become human in society and the kinds of societies we live in determine, in part, the kinds of human beings we become. Our educational system is a good illustration of what I mean here. Much of traditional education unfortunately still is carried on to fit children into the society. The virtues of obedience, loyalty, submission to authority, and discipline insure generation after generation of adults who do not question. The relationship between early conditioning and what we came to know of human nature reinforces and supports the society that gave rise to it.

In reflecting on the connection between human virtues and the society that fosters them, Dorothee Söelle asks whether Christian training in obedience can be even partially responsible for the clear conscience of Nazi murderers whose defense was that they were only doing as they were told. As already noted, she writes out of her experience as a German theologian who lived through the atrocities of the Second World War and the subsequent war trials. She challenges:

> I suspect that we Christians today have the duty to criticize the entire concept of obedience, and that this criticism must be radical, simply because we do not know who God is and what God, at any given moment, wills.... We cannot remove ourselves from history if we wish to speak seriously about God. And in our Christian history of the 20th century, obedience has played a catastrophic role. Who forgets this background or conveniently pushes it aside and once more naively attempts to begin with obedience, as if it were merely a matter of obeying the right lord, has not learned a thing from the instruction of God called history.[19]

This "instruction of God called history" has taught us that culture plays a greater role than previously acknowledged in determining the kind of people we are. As we inherit the values of society and make them our own, they become part of our self definition. Often, we are unaware of the underside of some of the values that we absorb into our being, so that, for example, Christian obedience may lead to the Holocaust or My Lai or Watergate or Irangate. Believing or doing what we are told is not in itself virtuous: It is not in itself Christian. Obedience is often a lack of courage and responsibility under the guise of virtue.

Another example of the effect of society in the development of human beings is violence in people's lives. Study after study shows that husbands who beat their wives were often themselves battered children. Some Vietnam veterans still suffer from nightmares and are prone to violent seizures because of their military training and experiences. Cases of multiple personalities have been traced to childhood experiences of sexual abuse. The only way to transform people is to transform the environment in which they live. It is not a case of either/or but of both/and.

Modern people make a distinction between nature created by God and culture created by human beings in a way that our forebears did not. We have come to understand that what we have known as history is only part of the story. We recognize that it is one view of the past, a view from the perspective of the powerful and victorious. Because of this we have developed a sense of responsibility for creating the future. Social patterns, past and present, are recognized as human products, not as God-given structures. As we strive to transform evil structures and customs in society, we not only are determining whether future generations will exist on this planet, we are also determining, in part, what kind of human beings they will be.

Tradition has often been interpreted to refer only to the past, but we have come to see it as that to which we are presently contributing. In theological terms, we may say that this understanding of history and human responsibility means that revelation is still occurring, that tradition is a process in which we are involved and that both revelation and tradition are dependent on the present, even as they are still dependent on the past. We are creating history; we are makers of tradition.

But if we are to create a new city, if we are to cooperate with the Spirit in renewing the face of the earth, then each of us is called both to personal conversion and to transform the structures of society as well. One or the other metanoia is not sufficient.

Of this metanoia, Buckley writes:

No mere static affirmation of the human and Christian
ideal of mutuality and equality is sufficient in order that
the Christian vision may at least be partly realized. Solid
and penetrating criticism of unjust structures, unjust personal relations and unjust history is essential. Repentance
for the individual Christian, repentance for the Church as
institution, repentance for society itself is a condition for
true growth.... Persons and structures are not what they
could be, but are sinful and unjust. Metanoia or conversion
is central for the individual person, for the Church (e.g., the
public confession of sorrow for the treatment of the Jewish
people voiced at Vatican II), central also for governments
and for society as a whole.[20]

We cannot emphasize too much that in order to enable wom-
en and men to become full human beings it will be necessary to
transform the social and cultural structures that are their context.
We do not become human in a vacuum. We need human contact,
not necessarily female or male contact. We have an ontological
vocation to be human. Simply because we exist, we are called to
be as fully as possible what we were created to be—human. But
that is possible only in a society that supports human growth.
We cannot define what it means to be human in isolation from
the cultural forces that impede or foster human development.

It seems to me that we do not yet know what it means to be
human. We have not created societies in which women and men
may develop to their fullest potential. We have not created structures that encourage human development. We have not even
provided the basic necessities for minimal existence for all wom-
en and men. Perhaps, in spite of all the scientific charts that
show us at the end of the evolutionary line or at the top of the
climb, we are only the missing link. It is difficult for us to imagine what full humanity may look like, but Paul tells us that
"the whole creation is eagerly waiting for God to reveal her
daughters and sons."[21]

Rosemary Ruether speaks of "redeemed humanity" when referring to the *basileia*, the time of God's reign on Earth:

> Redeemed humanity, reconnected with the *imago Dei*,
> means not only recovering aspects of our full psychic po-
> tential that have been repressed by cultural gender stereo-
> types, it also means transforming the way these capacities
> have been made to function socially.[22]

Ruether's way of saying that we do not yet know what it
means to be human is that there is nothing in our history that allows us to claim "a single model of redeemed humanity, as image of God, is something only partially disclosed under the
conditions of history. We seek it as a future self and world, still
not fully achieved, still not fully revealed."[23]

We have every reason to hope that this simultaneous transformation of persons and of society will contribute to the coming
of the *basileia*, when we will know the fullness of redemption.
Acknowledging that what people become is strongly influenced
by what culture has exposed them to, is not to deny free will; it
is, however, a call to heed what sociologists are pointing out
about the influence of cultural institutions and their effect on the
kinds of human beings we become. The age-old argument about
whether "we do what we are" or "we are what we do" must
now take into consideration the fact that we are, in part, what society has done to us.

The theologians of the Second Vatican Council hinted at the
link between personal transformation and the transformation of
society in the "Pastoral Constitution on the Church in the
Modern World." They wrote: "Just as human activity proceeds
from woman so is it ordered toward woman. For when a woman
works she not only alters things and society, she develops herself as well. She learns much, she cultivates her resources, she
goes outside of herself and beyond herself."[24] The mutual transformation of sinful humanity and evil structures will enable us
to go outside ourselves and beyond ourselves. In this journey we
may find not only ourselves and others, but we may finally find
God.

## Questions for Reflection

1. Read a magazine article on women or review magazine advertisements and try to determine if the author operates out of a dualistic or monistic anthropological pattern.

2. In your opinion, are there personality characteristics that are more appropriate for women than for men? If so, what are they and why are they more appropriate? If not, why do we set so many different restrictions for both boys and girls?

3. Do you think there are roles that are more appropriate for either sex? What are they?

4. Scientists tell us that we only use ten percent of our brain's power. What might children be like if they used fifteen percent? forty percent? ninety percent? What meaning will the word "adult" then take on?

## Endnotes

1. See Barbara Ehrenreich and Deidre English, *For Her Own Good: 150 Years of the Experts' Advice to Women* (New York: Doubleday, 1978) 128-130. Citation from W.C. Hall, *Sexual Knowledge* (Philadelphia: John C. Winston, 1916).

2. Thomas J. O'Brien, *An Advanced Catechism of Faith and Practice Based on the Third Plenary Council Catechism* (Chicago: The Oink Company, 1901) 7-8. (It was commonly called the Baltimore Catechism.)

3. *De Trinitate* 7.7,10.

4. *Summa Theologica* I,1,q.9,a,1.

5. *Malleus Malificarum* translated by Montague Summers (New York: Dover, 1971) 123. For further information on witch burnings see Mary Daly, *Gyn-Ecology* (Boston: Beacon Press, 1978) and Andrea Dworkin, *Woman Hating* (New York: E.P. Dutton, 1974).

6. *Malleus*, 116.

7. "Declaration of the Question of the Admission of Women to the Ministerial Priesthood," Sacred Congregation for the Doctrine of the Faith, (October 15, 1976) 27.

8. Quoted by Robert E. Burns, "Let's Put Women in Their Place" *U.S. Catholic*, July 1979, n.p.

9. Sara Butler, "Personhood, Sexuality and Complementarity and the Teaching of Pope John Paul II," *Chicago Studies* 32:1 (April 1993) 49.

10. *The Laws of Manu* translated by George Buhler (Delhi: Motilal Banarasidass, 1968) 193.

11. "Female-Male-Human," address given at Nijmegen, April 6, 1984 on the occasion of the inauguration of the Chair in Feminism and Christianity. This is the first chair of its kind in the world.

12. "On the Dignity and Vocation of Women," #21.

13. Mary Daly, *Pure Lust* (Boston: Beacon Press, 1984) 370.

14. Rosemary Radford Ruether, "A Religion for Women: Sources and Strategies," *Christianity and Crisis* (December 10, 1979) 309.

15. Ibid., 309.

16. New York: Morrow, 1939.

17. Halkes, "Female-Male-Human," 3.

18. Mary Buckley, "The Rising of the Woman is the Rising of the Race," *Journal of the Catholic Theological Society of America* 34 (1979) 48-63.

19. Dorothee Söelle, *Beyond Mere Obedience* (New York: Pilgrim Press, 1982) 10.

20. Buckley, "Rising of the Woman," 61-62.

21. Epistle to the Romans 8:19. The careful reader recognizes that I have taken the liberty to alter some of the language.

22. Rosemary Radford Ruether, *Sexism and God-Talk* (Boston: Beacon Press, 1983) 113.

23. Ibid., 114.

24. "Pastoral Constitution on the Church in the Modern World" 35. Let it be noted here that the bishops wrote "men" in each place where I have written "women." Since I presume that most of the readers are women and that it was the bishops' intention in the original statement to inspire their readers, I have translated the words in such a way that the full impact of the bishops, meaning may be felt by women. Such translations help us realize how much inspiration women have been deprived of because they have had to do mental gymnastics to include themselves in language that is exclusively male. It may also help men who read it understand women's arguments about inclusive language.

## 5

# Mary, the Mother of Jesus

Many years ago, the name Mary with all its derivatives was the most popular name for girls. There were Marias and Maureens, Mary Janes and Mary Ellens, not to mention Anne Maries and Rosemarys. But now Mary is not even in the top ten list of most popular names. It has been pushed aside by the Tracys and Tiffanys, the Kims and the Jennifers.

This is perhaps the greatest indication that devotion to Mary has fallen on hard times in North America. We do not find as many statues of Mary; the rosary is no longer among the most frequently said prayers; and novenas and devotions to Mary are all but unheard of in many places. Part of the reason for this is the changes that have occurred since the Second Vatican Council. But another part is also the result of women rejecting some of the things for which the image of Mary stood in other ages and which seem inappropriate in our own time. Popular novelist Mary Gordon speaks for many when she says, "For women like me, it was necessary to reject the image of Mary in order to hold onto the fragile hope of intellectual achievement, independence of identity, sexual fulfillment. Yet we were offered no alternative to this Marian image; hence, we were denied a po-

tent female image whose application was universal."[1] Gordon
clearly suggests here that a potent female image *is* possible.

Any discussion of Mary needs to take place on at least three
levels: history, dogma, and the symbolic level of popular tradition. Mary is not only a human person who existed in a particular time and place, she is also a strong symbol whose meaning
has been reclaimed by Christians in each culture and century according to their own lights. What we believe about Mary often
has little to do with the Jewish mother of two thousand years
ago and a great deal to do with visions, apparitions, and traditions of the ages. Often it is not the woman of Nazareth who is
venerated but the Lady of Lourdes or Knock or Guadalupe. We
shall speak of Mary as symbol and Mary of the popular piety later in this chapter, but first let us look at what we know of Mary,
the first century young Jewish woman of whom we speak.

In this chapter, we will discuss the historical Mary, as known
to us through scripture, two dogmas that have been promulgat-
ed in modern times, and the symbolic role played by Mary
through the ages that gives rise to popular devotion. In each case
we will consider these issues in the light of feminist thought.

### Mary in Scripture

We know very little about the historical Mary in spite of the
fact that all four evangelists include her in one or another in-
cident in Jesus' life.[2] Matthew and Luke tell us stories of the infancy of Jesus, but Matthew does not make Mary a central figure.
The angel comes to Joseph, the genealogy of Jesus is traced
through Joseph's line; Joseph is the main initiator of action. Mary
plays a passive role; she was engaged, was found with child,
was received into Joseph's home, was found by the wise men.
Twice we are told that "Joseph got up and took the child and his
mother," once when they escaped from Herod into Egypt and
again when it was time to return to Nazareth. Active voice is not
used in reference to Mary. Others act upon her; she remains passive and docile.

Luke presents a different picture. The angel comes to Mary;
she is the one who is consulted and who gives consent to the angel's request. At no time are we told that she stopped to ask per-

mission from Joseph, her mother, or the chief priests of the temple. In this gospel, Mary is an independent agent cooperating with God in the redemption of the world.

Having heard from the angel that her aged cousin Elizabeth is also pregnant, Mary sets out to the hill country to help her. Again, we are not told that she asked permission, but rather: "Thereupon Mary set out proceeding in haste into the hill country to a town of Judah." The woman Elizabeth is filled with the Holy Spirit and recognizes Mary as "the mother of my Lord." We have only to read Mary's words in the Magnificat to gain an understanding of Mary as an active theological agent in her own right. She proclaims: "All ages to come shall call me blessed. God, you who are mighty, have done great things for me. Holy is your name."[3] The rest of the Magnificat indicates that Mary had a strong sense of what we in this day call social consciousness. Listen to the words: "God has deposed the mighty from their thrones and raised the lowly to high places. The hungry, God has given every good thing while the rich God has sent empty away" (Lk 1:52–53).

If Luke set Mary as central character, Mark (whose gospel was the first written and who does not include an infancy narrative) is not so kind. In the scene which we will speak of here, some translations of his gospel do not mention Mary directly but speak of the relatives of Jesus and leave us with the decision whether or not Mary is to be counted among them. Other translations, however, put her in the picture.

Jesus went home with his newly chosen Twelve and such a great crowd gathered that he could not even get a bite to eat. Then, Mark tells us: "When his family heard of this they came to take charge of him, saying, "he is out of his mind." Mark sandwiches in a discussion with some scribes who charge that Jesus is possessed by Beelzebub and that he casts out demons by the power of the prince of demons. The whole scene is cast in negative tones so that when the disciples tell Jesus that his mother and brothers are outside, he replies, "Who are my mother and brothers?" And gazing around him at those seated in the circle, he continued, "These are my mother and brothers. Whoever does the will of God is brother and sister and mother to me"

(3:21–35). The Marcan context with Jesus' family thinking him crazy and the scribes thinking him possessed by demons "considerably sharpens the meaning of 3:31–35, and for Mark the natural family seems to be replaced by an eschatological family that is inside 'the house' with Jesus—'house' being a possible reference to the church."[4]

In another place, Mark proposes that Jesus did not work any miracles in Nazareth because "No prophet is without honor except in his native place, among his own kindred and in his own house" (6:4). Mark makes no effort to remove Mary from these negative overtones. We have no assurance that Mark perceived Mary to be a believer, a disciple of Jesus.

Both Luke and Matthew use the story differently. Before we speak to that issue, it may be well for us to once more recall that the gospels are not biographies of Jesus but faith statements, and each represents the theological viewpoint of the particular writer. Neither Matthew nor Luke refer to "his own," who, thinking Jesus crazy, who come to take him away, and Luke even gives an excuse why Jesus' mother and brothers are outside the house while the disciples are inside; they could not get near him because of the crowd, thus suggesting that they were not excluded from the disciples.

All three evangelists agree on what is involved in discipleship. "Luke's notion of what constitutes discipleship and makes one a member of Jesus' eschatological family is not much different from the notion of Mark and Matthew: namely, obedience to God. Luke, however, is much clearer than Mark and Matthew in insisting that Jesus' mother and brothers meet the criterion."[5] Luke makes only one mention of Mary in the Acts of the Apostles. She gathered in prayer with the eleven apostles and the unnamed women in the upper room after the ascension of Jesus. Most biblical scholars agree that it was this group plus the newly elected Matthias who were present on the day of Pentecost when the Holy Spirit came down upon the new church.

Of the four evangelists, only John never calls her by name; she is "the mother of Jesus." John is also the only one to tell the story of the marriage feast at Cana. In this scene, Mary assumes a role of authority and ignores Jesus' "Woman, how does this concern of yours involve me? My hour is not yet come." She does not argue with him, or plead, but merely instructs the waiters to do whatever Jesus tells them (Jn 2:4–5). Like the virgin birth, this story has more to do with Christology than with Mariology. "The story pertains in some way to the 'hour of Jesus,' the water intended for the Jewish rites of purification has been replaced by a wine that is better than any hitherto offered—a wine that by its quality and perhaps even by its abundance reveals to Jesus' disciples in a wedding setting the glory of Jesus."[6] The disciples believe in him and now begin to see his glory manifested.

One significant note is that Jesus calls Mary "Woman" not "Mother," as he does also at the crucifixion. It was not a common way for a son to address his mother but it was also the way Jesus addressed the Samaritan woman and Mary Magdalen. This may point to the fact that Jesus places no special emphasis on the physical relationship with Mary. "This interpretation...would bring John into agreement with the synoptic gospels where, as we saw, a family of disciples takes precedence over the natural family and its claims."[7] John is the only evangelist to place Mary at the crucifixion. Just as he does not call her by name, he leaves the Beloved Disciple nameless. Their anonymity serves to focus primary interest on their symbolic importance. Thus Jesus ties Mary with the small community of disciples as Mother.

> In giving the beloved disciple to Mary as her son, and Mary to the disciple as his mother, Jesus brought into existence a new community of believing disciples, the same "eschatological family" which appears in the synoptic gospels ...Mary, who in the Cana episode had been distinguished from the disciples, now becomes the mother of the disciple *par excellence,* and so becomes herself a model of belief and discipleship.[8]

It would be a mistake, however, to suggest that Mary, the Mother of Jesus, is a central figure in John's gospel. The woman who is central is she who was the first witness of the resurrection, Mary from Magdala. She is also the only woman named in all four gospels. We shall speak more of Magdalen in Chapter 8.

### Marian Doctrines

There are three main beliefs about Mary that are held by the Catholic Church besides the doctrine that she is the Mother of God; they are: Mary's virginity, the Immaculate Conception, and the Assumption. The question concerning whether or not Mary is to be called the Mother of God was settled by the Council of Ephesus (431) in spite of Nestorius' argument that she be called only the Mother of Christ. The dogmas which we will discuss here are the Immaculate Conception and the Assumption.[9] More will be said about the virginity of Mary in a subsequent section.

### The Immaculate Conception

People often confuse the virgin birth, which has to do with the intervention of God in the birth of Jesus, and the Immaculate Conception, which has to do with Mary's conception by her parents whom tradition names Anne and Joachim. The belief in the Immaculate Conception was proclaimed a dogma in 1854 by Pius IX but that was not the beginning of the belief.

Even in Augustine's time, the view was held that Mary was preserved from sin. Theologians have argued both sides of the issue through the ages. Anselm held that the most one could say was that Mary was sanctified in her mother's womb and so preserved from actual sin. Underlying Augustine's theory is the idea that the sexual act itself is always at least venially sinful and that it is the means of transmitting original sin. Given this starting point, it makes sense, he argues, to conclude that Mary was immaculately conceived, that is, conceived without sin. This doctrine does not suggest that Mary was conceived in a different way than all of us were conceived—through the physical union of our mothers and fathers.

Bernard of Clairvaux (d. 1153) was perhaps the most influential medieval theologian regarding Mariology. In spite of his sermons and writings honoring Mary and in spite of his great devotion to her as the "mediator with the Mediator," Bernard opposed the doctrine of the Immaculate Conception. For him it was enough that Mary was sanctified in her mother's womb and that she remained sinless throughout her life. Bernard opposed the doctrine because he did not find support for it in the bible or in the works of the early fathers of the church. (He probably did not know of the works of St. John of Damascus.) He also held Augustine's view of original sin. He asks, "How could there be sanctity without the sanctifying spirit, or how could the Holy Spirit be in any way associated with sin? Or how could sin not have been present where concupiscence was not absent?"[10]

It was St. Bernard who popularized the belief that Mary is the aqueduct through which God has chosen to bestow all blessings on humanity. Christ was seen as a stern judge from whom sinners needed protection. Mary it was who provided that loving protection by her compassionate intercession with God. It was at this time that legends grew recounting Mary's ability to save even the worst sinners who had devotion to her. If they were refused entry into heaven through the front door, she would sneak them in through the back.

In the thirteenth century, Thomas Aquinas and Bonaventure both had reservations concerning the doctrine because if Mary were sinless she did not need Christ's redemption. According to this logic, it also followed that Mary would not have to die since death was thought to be a punishment for the sin of our first parents. In this regard, it was Duns Scotus who stated that the mediation of Christ is not belittled by Mary's sinlessness but rather enhanced by it since prevention is better than cure.

By the eighteenth century, a distinction was made between Mary's active conception by her parent's sexual act and her passive conception, the infusion of her soul by God. By nature of the first, she was conceived in sin, but by the merits of Christ, applied to her in advance, the results of sin were prevented from taking effect.

Some may find it disturbing to discover that doctrines of the church have a long and sometimes stormy history. We must remind ourselves that God did not act once and for all on this planet two thousand years ago, but rather God is constantly acting with us and enabling us to search out the theological truth in the beliefs of the Christian tradition. We need to discover today in this twentieth century what the belief in the sinlessness of Mary has to say to us. Recall that the Catholic Church, which among all the other Christian denominations has most fostered devotion to Mary, has never relied only on scripture but on scripture and tradition—tradition being that process whereby the Christian community discovers ever anew the meaning of the doctrines we have inherited.

What may be most significant for women today is that, through the doctrine of the Immaculate Conception, the privilege of Jesus, sinlessness, was extended to one just like us, to a woman.

Carol Frances Jagen, B.V.M., calls our attention to the significance of Mary as patron of the United States under the title of the Immaculate Conception. Drawing on the popular depiction of Mary as the woman of Genesis 3 crushing the head of the serpent, Jagen moves from the personal level to the societal order and asks whether the Immaculate Conception, as a symbol of human freedom not bound by sin, may call us forth in the struggle for justice and peace. "Can the Immaculate Conception be our symbol of human freedom from the power of evil wherever it exists? Can the Immaculate Conception become a vital symbol of the power of God's love, freely accepted and operative in our lives? ...New meanings for this symbol must be interiorized and made operative in the minds and hearts of people of faith, young and old."[11] I would suggest that the reader consult Jagen's book, *Mary According to a Woman*, for a fuller discussion of the connection between the Immaculate Conception, freedom, and the responsibility for social justice.

### The Assumption

Carl Jung called the promulgation of the dogma of the Assumption one of the most significant religious developments since the Reformation.[12] It is important because of what it says in its implicit denial of a dualistic way of thinking about the separation of soul and body and the value of the one over the other. Mary's whole being was taken to heaven. It is the promise of our own assumption/resurrection. Mary's assumption is a foreshadowing, a promise of what we can expect because of our faith in Christ.

There is no scriptural basis for belief in the assumption of Mary, but from early times, apocryphal literature speaks of the falling asleep of Mary and the finding of her empty tomb by the disciples. Mary's assumption means that she is the first of the saints to participate in the resurrection of Jesus. It is an affirmation of the resurrection of the body, not merely of the immortality of the soul. Mary is no longer just an historic personage but is established above time and space in a transcendent realm. She is now a focus of our prayer and devotion.

Again, we must remember that the main concern of any of the beliefs that we hold is what can they tell us about God and about our relationship and responsibility to God. We ought not hold any doctrine superstitiously or reject it cavalierly. We must always search it for the meaning it holds; for the revelation it may bestow about the God whom Jesus called Abba.

When Pope Pius XII announced the dogma in 1950, he was responding to at least one hundred years of requests from Catholics of all walks of life. A careful reading of the words of *Munificentissimus Deus* unearths the significance of this belief.

> We also hope that, while materialistic theories and the moral corruption arising from them are threatening to extinguish the light of virtue, and by stirring up strife, to destroy the lives of men and women, the exalted destiny of both our soul and body may in this striking manner be brought clearly to the notice of all men and women. Finally, it is our hope that faith in the bodily Assumption of Mary into heaven may make our faith in our own resurrection both stronger and more active.[13]

### Mary in Popular Tradition

Though we know very little of the historical Mary, we do have a rich tradition about her as a Christian symbol who has taken on many faces over the ages. Raymond Brown maintains that "precisely because we do not know much about the historical character and individuality of Mary, she lends herself more freely than Jesus does to a symbolic trajectory. She has been adaptable in various times and places, establishing a relationship between the ministry of Jesus and what it means to be a Christian later and elsewhere."[14]

Through the ages, Mary has taken on symbolic meanings that

have been significant to the particular religious climate of the day. St. Athanasius and Coptic writers describe Mary as the perfect Egyptian nun who ate and slept only when her body demanded, who spoke in modulated tones, who avoided family and talk of the world. After the Edict of Constantine in 313, Christians were no longer martyred and persecuted. They were free to develop other means of living out their faith; other ways of proving the tenacity of their belief in Jesus. Many women and men took to the desert and lived lives of great penance. Asceticism replaced martyrdom as the sign of special election. Mary became the role model for the thousands of women who chose eremitic lives.

During the Middle Ages, Mary the Jewish mother of the first century became "Our Lady," protector of the knights who rode in her name and under her banner. This was a period of erotic excesses among the nobility; romantic love was glorified in songs, poems, stories, and dramas. Courtiers, musicians, and poets spoke of secret loves between women of high rank and knights of the court. A symbol of chaste love was needed and it was found in Mary.

Mary of the Renaissance is a tender mother caring for her children. One good example of the image of Mary during this period is on display in the Gardner Museum in Boston. An enamel plaque attributed to the Limoges craftsman Nardon Penicauld presents the Virgin and Child surrounded by angels carrying banners with Mary's virtues spelled out. Charity appears (but not faith and hope); and prudence (but not justice or fortitude). Humility, patience, obedience, purity, truth, and poverty help fill out the image.[15] The art of every age both reveals and creates common beliefs of that age. It draws from the popular symbols while at the same time reenforcing them. Penicauld illustrates what the symbol of Mary was in that era: the saintly Mother, ever watchful of her children, surrounded by the virtues that were encouraged in women in their role as mother.

Most devotions honoring Mary do not honor her as the woman of Nazareth but rather in symbolic roles as the Lady of such places as Lourdes, Fatima, Knock, or Guadalupe, and more recently, Medjugorje. Throughout history Marian devotion has had a great deal to do with apparitions and visions. Each culture, each time and place claims and reclaims the symbols of Christianity according to its own lights. For example, Brazilian theologians Ivone Gebara and Maria Clara Bingemer[16] situate the apparition of Our Lady of Guadalupe to Juan Diego in the context of how Mary's symbolism had previously served in Latin America. Mary had been presented as the protector of the conquistadors against the Indians who were regarded as infidels. After bloody battles in which the indigenous culture was destroyed, the dominant image of Mary made it possible for Fray Antonio Maria to say, "No one can doubt that the conquest was successful because of the Queen of the Angels!"[17] Gebara and Bingemer contend that because the conquistadors, especially the missionaries, thought they were unique possessors of the truth, and because they did not recognize their own limitations in language, culture, and education, they were unable to grasp the depth of the spirituality of the Indians. Our Lady of Guadalupe changed all that.

In the period of the wars of independence in Latin America, Mary was on the side of the liberators. She was a "general" in the army of José de San Martin, and her image was carried into battle by Símon Bólivar. After independence, she was declared patron of the various countries. In both cases, the conquistadors and the liberators, devotion to Mary mirrored the ideology of the believers. Her symbol provided religious legitimation to each of the causes. This point can not be ignored in any discussion of popular devotion and especially of appearances.

The significance of Mary's appearance to Juan Diego was that Mary stood on the side of the Indians. She looked like an Indian woman, she spoke their language, and she requested that a chapel be built. "This means she wants to have a dwelling on Indian soil; she wants to be an Indian."[18]

The image of Our Lady of Guadalupe has survived even until today as a means of revealing and reinforcing the faith of the Indians. In this case, as in the case of the conquistadors and the liberators, the symbol legitimizes a particular cause. It raises the question for us about how we use our symbols and what they are legitimating.

### Reclaiming Traditional Titles of Mary

When we change our thought patterns, we begin to notice shadows not seen before and lights not previously recognized. In each of the interpretations of the symbol of Mary just mentioned, some image of Mary was rejected and another developed that spoke to the life and times of the people. In our own day, women are beginning to notice the shadow side of the titles Handmaid, Virgin, and Mother as they have been applied to Mary and as they have been presented as models for women. Kari Børresen speaks for many when she maintains: "The figure of Mary is a patriarchal construct: virgin, wife, mother, and adjunct to the male. She embodies the essential connection between femininity and subordination forged by the patriarchal mind-set. To make her the model for free women is absurd, until that connection is broken."[19]

*Handmaid, Mother, Virgin*[20]    Mary, the self-proclaimed "handmaid of the Lord," has been held up as the ideal of humility, lowliness, blind obedience, forgetfulness of self, and docility. There is a danger when these "passive" virtues become the province of only one portion of the population—the poor, the servant class, or women, or others whom society identifies as lesser. When powerful peoples define them as lesser, as not worthy of respect, or as second class, the poor, servants, and women begin to interiorize these judgments and to believe that they are not worthy of the care, the service, or the respect they are called upon to give others.

Historically, as Mary's cult grew in particular areas, the condition of women worsened. In countries where devotion to Mary is strongest, women appear to be among the most oppressed. Wife beating, lack of legal rights and protection of the law, as well as a general attitude that men and boys are more valuable than women and girls are the most common manifestations of this oppression.

But are these the only lessons we can learn from the role of Mary as the handmaid of the Lord? I think not. If we remember that when Mary said, "Behold the handmaid of the Lord. Let it be done unto me as you say," she immediately went to visit her cousin Elizabeth. There she sang the words:

My being proclaims the greatness of the Lord, my spirit finds joy in God my savior, For God has looked upon this servant in her lowliness; all ages to come shall call me blessed. God who is mighty has done great things for me, Holy is God's name.

These words do not suggest that Mary had a sense of herself as unworthy in comparison to others or that she was somehow more lowly than Elizabeth whom she has come to help; but they sing out a relationship with God that is appropriate for all Christians, not just for women. Mary's Magnificat then proceeds to suggest God's action in the world as confusing the proud in their inmost thoughts, as deposing the mighty, as raising up the lowly, as feeding the hungry—actions that God does not take without the cooperation of courageous, active disciples.

*Mary as Virgin*    The second title traditionally bestowed on Mary is that of Virgin. The traditional symbols, including Mary herself, define and describe all of reality from the perspective of the dominant shapers of society. Henry Adams may have said it best in his essay "The Dynamo and the Virgin": "Symbol or energy, the Virgin had acted as the greatest force the Western world ever felt and had drawn man's activities to herself more strongly than any other power, natural or supernatural, had ever done."[21] It cannot be denied that the myth of Mary the Virgin encouraged men to win wars, build cathedrals, and to create magnificent art, poetry, and music; but we are only now coming to realize that it has had deleterious effects on women. The Virgin on a pedestal is merely a religious expression of the attitude that helped bind the feet of Chinese women and imposed *purdah* on Moslem women. They all treat women as objects, to be restricted, guarded so that they may better serve men.

Be that as it may, the doctrine of the virginity of Mary refers to the belief that Jesus was conceived by the power of the Holy Spirit without the intervention of a human father. As such, it is more a statement about Jesus than it is about Mary. It reminds us that Jesus was one with God from the first moment of his human existence. He did not grow into becoming divine. Like other doctrines, this one is a matter of theology, not biology. The im-

portant concern is not whether Mary had intercourse, but whether Jesus is Divine.

As defined by the early fathers of the church, the virgin Eve
was misled by an angel and disobeyed God, thereby contributing to the fall of all humanity. Salvation came about when a
second virgin received the word of an angel and obeyed God's
word. Few scripture scholars today would hold Eve more responsible than Adam in the Genesis myth, but this is a topic for
chapter seven.

Tertullian rejected the "doctrine of the unbroken hymen" because it suggested a Gnostic view that Jesus did not have a real
physical body but only a spiritual one that could pass through
the walls of the womb without opening it. St. Jerome, on the other hand saw an analogy between the virgin birth and the Risen
Christ passing through closed doors. It is he who worked out an
exegesis that made cousins of the "brothers and sisters of the
Lord" (Mk 6:3; Mt 13:55–56). Jerome operated out of a theology
that considered the body evil and sexual intercourse debasing,
even in marriage. He wanted to defend the absolute superiority
of virginity and thus presented Mary as the symbol of un-
blemished virginity.

According to Raymond Brown, it is possible that in the earliest Christian tradition, the idea that God specifically intervened
in Jesus' conception and birth did not exclude the fatherhood of
Joseph. Hebrew scriptures, like other classical literature, commonly suggest a man's greatness by the intervention of God in
his birth. Myths surrounded the births of many great men. Think
of the birth of Moses, of Isaac, of Samuel, and of Alexander the
Great.

Some of today's feminists are reclaiming the ancient meaning
of the word "virgin." The virgin, in ancient writings was she
who was complete in herself, she who did not receive her definition from another; whose being was not owned by a man—lord,
father, lover, or spouse. The Goddesses Athena, Diana, and Kore
were virgins in spite of their sexual activity. This is not to place
Mary in that pantheon, but rather to challenge our conceptions
about the significance of the meaning of virginity. I repeat, the
question is more one of theology than of biology.

As asceticism flourished in the early church, it was accompanied by a negative view of matter (especially the female human body), which marked Gnostic belief.

> Correlatively, in the light of the growing ascetic ideal of virginity also related at this time to an anti-flesh bias, the evils of sex were particularly identified with the female. The resulting powerful aversion of Christian male thinkers to female sexuality gave added impetus to the honoring of Mary for her uniqueness in having conceived virginally, that is, for the non-use of her sexuality vis-a-vis a man, and to the corresponding belittling of women who exercised their sexuality.[22]

What is significant for us today is that virginity calls our attention to the dignity and majesty of the human body in itself. A woman's body is not important, not sacred because of its relationship with a man or children; it is, in itself, sacred, a temple, complete. It suggests to us that a woman's total identity need not depend on what she does or does not do with her body.

*Mary as Mother*    Mary as Mother of God has been honored in music, art, architecture, and theology. The shadow side of this devotion has not received much attention until recently. We will now look at two negative consequences of the veneration that has been given to Mary as Mother. The first is the unreal expectations imposed upon mothers by the model of the perfect Mother Mary. Emphasis on Mary as Mother reinforces the notion that motherhood is the divinely ordained vocation for women. Motherhood is not only seen as the primary vocation of women, it is a call to a life where a good mother "never thinks of herself; is always there when I need her." Perfect motherhood is an impossible challenge for mothers of all ages.

The second negative consequence of the image of Mary as Mother has to do with the encouragement of a childlike attitude among Christians. A study of Marian hymns reveals that Christians are kept in a childlike dependent attitude toward Mary, depending upon her as a little child depends upon its mother. It is as if we are waiting for Mary to convince God to act in our behalf, even as one parent (mother or father) might convince the other on behalf of a child. This is a two-pronged message. On the one hand it illustrates our utter dependence on God, but on the other, it encourages a lack of responsibility toward transforming the face of the earth. If we passively wait for God to act without assuming responsibility, we indeed act as children and not as the mature adult Christians described by the American Bishops in their 1980 pastoral, "The Laity: Called and Gifted":

> One of the chief characteristics of all men and women to-day is their sense of being adult members of the same church.... Laymen and women feel themselves called to exercise the same mature independence and particular self direction which characterize them in other areas of life.... The adult character of the people of God flows from Baptism and Confirmation which are the foundations of the Christian life and ministry.

The title of Mother, of course, is not entirely negative. After pondering the question from various sides, we may be ready to articulate a theology of motherhood that is truly Christian and liberating for both children and mothers alike. Yet we must remember that when the woman in the crowd called out "Blessed is the womb that bore thee and the breasts that gave thee suck," Jesus replied that blessedness lay more in hearing the word of God and keeping it. Mary, like all other disciples of Jesus, is blessed because of her response to God, not because of her biological motherhood. Elizabeth Johnson suggests that we might better use "sister" for Mary. Of course that would then free up the title of "Mother" for God.

### Model for Liberated Women

Our own times have prompted the American Bishops to refer to Mary as a model for liberated women. In their pastoral, *Behold Your Mother*, they write, "The dignity which Christ's redemption won for all women was fulfilled uniquely in Mary as the model of all feminine freedom."[23] Wonderful as that may sound, it still holds that there may be a different way for women to be

Christian than for men. I would also question the accuracy of the claim that honor bestowed on Mary mirrors the dignity accorded to women.

There appears to be a consensus growing that Mary may provide a more appropriate model for us as "Disciple." She is being reclaimed by those who understand their Christianity as a challenge to action on behalf of justice; who believe that following Christ has to do with the rejection of systems of domination, of violence and of disrespect for Earth and the creatures with whom we share it. Mary as Disciple may be the symbol we have been searching for.

Let us consider for a moment the importance of symbols in our religious enterprise. Having repudiated some of the traditional symbols, we have been existing in a symbolic vacuum. When the symbols that may have had meaning in another age no longer speak to us in the same way, we reject them as representative of values that are no longer cherished by our society. Women are reappropriating and redefining traditional Christian symbols, and they are beginning to communicate something different than they did a few short years ago. This reclamation illustrates the symbol's ability to bring together our Christian tradition, the values of our society, and our own experience.

Just as Avery Dulles rethought his five models of church and saw them all fulfilled in the model of disciple, there is a growing movement to subsume all of Mary's titles under that of Disciple. As Disciple, Mary is then symbol not only for women, but for all Christians and for the church itself.

We now perceive that in every age the church has made contemporary the symbol of discipleship. In the words of Paul VI:

> The Virgin Mary has always been proposed to the faithful by the church as an example to be imitated not precisely in the type of life she led, and much less for the socio-cultural background in which she lived and which today scarcely exists anywhere. Rather, she is held up as an example to the faithful for the way in which in her own particular life she fully and responsibly accepted the will of God, because she heard the word of God and acted on it, and because

charity and a spirit of service were the driving force of her actions. She is worthy of imitation because she was the first and most perfect of Christ's disciples.[24]

### Questions for Reflection

1. What images of Mary are positive for you? Which are negative?

2. Is your devotion (or lack or devotion) to Mary more dependent on scripture or on visions such as Lourdes or Knock? Why do you think this is so?

3. How would you present Mary as a model for young women today?

4. How would you explain the theological significance of the Immaculate Conception to an adult education class? How would you explain the Assumption?

5. How do you feel about combining all of Mary's titles under the title of Disciple?

### Endnotes

1. Mary Gordon, "Coming to Terms With Mary," *Commonweal*, January 25, 1982, 179.

2. Raymond Brown, Karl P. Donfried, Joseph Fitzmyer, John Reumann, *Mary in the New Testament* (Philadelphia: Fortress Press, 1978).

3. The translation is from *Psalms Anew: A Non-Sexist Edition* by Maureen Leach, OSF and Nancy Schreck, OSF (Dubuque, Iowa: Sisters of St. Francis, 1984).

4. Brown, *Mary*, 58-59.

5. Ibid., 168.

6. Ibid., 187.

7. Ibid., 189.

8. Ibid., 66.

9. The material in this section is taken from Hilda Graef, *Mary: History of Doctrine and Devotion*, Vols. I and II (New York: Sheed and Ward, 1963, 1965) and Marina Warner, *Alone of All Her Sex* (New York: Alfred Knopf, 1976).

10. Letter to the Canons of Lyons, quoted by Graef, 236.

11. Carol Frances Jagen, B.V.M., *Mary According to a Woman* (Kansas City: Leaven Press, 1985) 157.

12. C.G. Jung, *The Answer to Job* translated by R.F.C. Hull (London: 1954). Quoted by Warner, 132.

13. nn. 49-51. Quoted in Graef, vol II, 147.

14. Raymond Brown, *Biblical Reflections on Crises Facing the Church* (New York: Paulist Press, 1975) 106.

15. Marina Warner, *Alone of All Her Sex*, 185. The material on Mary as symbol is from Warner, and Raymond Brown, *Biblical Reflections*.

16. Ivone Gebara and Maria Clara Bingemer, *Mary, Mother of God, Mother of the Poor* (Maryknoll: Orbis Books, 1989) 128-154.

17. Quoted in Gebara and Bingemer, *Mother of God*, 129.

18. Ibid., 153.

19. Kari Børressen, "Mary in Catholic Theology" in *Mary in the Churches* (Concilium, 168) edited by Hans Küng and Jürgen Moltmann (New York: Seabury, 1983) 54-55.

20. For a fuller discussion of this topic, see Elizabeth Johnson, "The Marian Tradition and the Reality of Women" *Horizons* 12/1 (1985).

21. Henry Adams, "The Dynamo and the Virgin" in *The Education of Henry Adams* (Boston: Houghton Mifflin, 1961) 388-389.

22. Johnson, *The Marian Tradition*, 123.

23. National Council of Catholic Bishops, November 21, 1973.

24. *Marialis Cultis*, February, 1974. #35.

# 6

# Sin, Grace, and Morality

Christians have a well defined vocabulary for sin. We speak of mortal sin, venial sin, actual sin, original sin, capital sins, sins of omission, sins of commission, and occasions of sin. More than a third of the old Baltimore Catechism explained the many and myriad ways that we humans have thought of sinning. Sin has been a "big category" theologically for us and with good reason. The events of daily life, personally, interpersonally, nationally, and internationally give strong witness to the force of evil in our world.

Recent changes in our thoughts about sin have led some to accuse our age of having lost a sense of sin. I don't think this is so. We have developed a different sense of sin. We have come to realize that sin is not so easy to define; that extenuating circumstances need to be taken into consideration; that sin can not be tallied, measured, and counted, like a shopping list. We have even become aware of sins of which we were formerly unconscious or unwilling to admit to.

While the liberation theologies, including feminist theologies, have focused attention on the hidden faces of sin, two other contributions, one positive and the other negative, also add to this new understanding. The first is the explosion of psychological and sociological knowledge in our century. These new sciences have provided insights into human development that shed light on the theological discussion of good and evil.

The second is the involvement of Christians in the Holocaust. The devastating and overwhelming evil in the structure of Christian society forced us to reevaluate our concept of sin. We were forced to examine our responsibility for the inhuman tragedy that was Nazism. Like racism and sexism in our own society, Nazism flourished in a society that identified itself as Christian. Moreover, nothing was done to the Jews that the church had not already done in the past two thousand years; the scale was greater, but persecution because of Jewishness has a long Christian history. Prayers condemning the "perfidious Jews" and teaching that the Jews killed Jesus, kept the flame of hatred burning from generation to generation. Little was done in the churches to educate the people, to form consciences, to eliminate prejudice.

In this chapter I will discuss some of the changes in our thinking about sin in general and investigate how these developments have affected feminist notions of sin. The developments that I will examine here are: 1) the tension between individual sin and systemic sin; 2) the tension between virtue and vice; and 3) the tension between law and relationships. In each case I speak of tension, not of denying the reality of the one in favor of the other. It is not a case of either/or but of both/and.

### Tension Between Individual and Social Sin

In the course of the past twenty centuries, we have lost the impact of the prophetic nature of the scriptures. We have domesticated them, privatized them, perhaps even trivialized them. The strength and power of the message of the prophets and the vitality and potency of the preaching of Jesus have been diluted, sweetened, and sentimentalized so that they are no longer recognizable. In the process, we have sometimes pinched and constricted the notion of sin to cover trivial issues and used our energy in nit-picking about personal idiosyncracies that might better have come under the umbrella of good manners or civilized behavior. In Roman Catholicism, the practice of private confession, usually in a dark and anonymous box, while protective of person's psyche and reputation, also reinforced the private character of sin.

Focusing on intimate and personal sin kept other forms of sin in the background. Communications experts have discovered that the public consciousness is only three issues wide. When the evening news introduces a new crisis or catastrophe, last night's concern is almost forgotten. In the same way, when we concentrate our energies on minor infractions and failings, we have neither the time nor the energy to address more serious shortcomings. When I was a young sister, a measure of how obedient, and therefore how good, was how many pins one wore in her veil. Three were permitted, and the understanding was "she that is faithful in that which is least is faithful in that which is greater." This may have been true for others, but it did not hold true for me. The time, psychic energy, and attention spent on the issue of pins distracted me from more significant issues. Besides, I was left with guilt, half believing that perhaps if I were faithful in least things I may have somehow learned to be faithful in the greater; but I never had a chance to think of the greater, too busy was I with the least. My students know that my shorthand, "three-pin syndrome," translates to "think big."

One issue that consumes our attention (so that we cannot see other issues) is human sexuality. When the predominant or exclusive metaphor for sin is sex, injustice, domination, and violence can more easily be ignored. Anne E. Patrick warns that:

> ...moral theology and pastoral practice emphasizing sexual sins contribute to neurotic patterns of individual behavior as well as to social injustice. With the rest of life removed from the arena of sin and grace, the injustice of social systems and cultural values never comes to attention.[1]

I am not suggesting that sex may not become a source of sin, but it is certainly not the whole story. Attending to systemic sin is not a denial of personal sin. One does not negate the other; in fact, each is witness to the other.

The interaction of sociology, psychology, and theology has turned the spotlight on sinful systems in society. Systemic sin is not a new discovery, a new sin. It has always been around, but we have not paid sufficient attention to it. We have not "named" it, and "nameless" it has been more difficult to recognize. Systemic sin is that sin which exists in the structures, institutions, customs, and laws of society. It is the sin for which no individual tends to feel responsible because it is the result of decisions, judgments, and actions of so many. It is the sin that results when reverence and respect for the human beings involved is missing. It is easy for us in this century to admit that slavery is a sinful system; it was not always so obvious. Thomas Aquinas made a case for the existence of slaves and the Vatican upheld slavery even after the American Civil War. Something in the culture of Aquinas and the nineteenth-century popes, something in their lives blinded them to the reality that seems so clear to us. But they are not judged by our insights, nor are we to be judged by theirs. In every age we are responsible for what has been called culpable ignorance. Lack of knowledge resulting from the circumstances of our lives and the time and place in which we live, does not leave us guilty. However, lack of knowledge that is the result of our own disinterest or selfishness does not eliminate or mitigate our responsibility.

We are responsible to the wisdom of our own age, and that wisdom has identified such evils as oppressive governments, communism, capitalism, consumerism, and the destruction of natural resources as sin. Racism and sexism are only now being recognized as pervasive sins in most societies. What marks such societies is the definition of some people as subordinate to others and the assignment of characteristics and roles to the subordinates that benefit the powerful. The American Catholic bishops have admitted to the sins of racism and sexism that have infected and still infect the church itself.

Since racism and sexism are so overwhelmingly prevalent, we are often as blind to them as we are to pollution. It may be well, therefore, to spell out just what is meant by these twin evils. Racism is a belief that race is the primary determinant of human characteristics, traits, abilities, and talents, and that racial differences produce an inherent superiority of a particular race. Similarly, sexism is a belief that sex is the primary determinant of human characteristics, traits, abilities, and talents, and that sexual differences produce an inherent superiority of a particular sex. According to this definition, both Blacks and whites may be racists; both men and women may be sexist. Black supremacists as well as white supremacists are racist. Female separatist groups as well as male groups and institutions may be sexist.

Unfortunately, some people of color and women, defined by the dominant society as lesser, suffer the added tragedy of believing the above definitions. They believe that their abilities, talents, and characteristics are determined by virtue of being born Black or female. They have internalized the definition assigned to them by the dominant society. The oppressors live within them. They believe that the popular myth is true: They are lesser. According to the definition above, victims, too, can be racist. What needs to be eliminated then is both the self hatred that victims feel and the hatred of the other that racists feel.

Rosemary Radford Ruether maintains that to locate a certain reality as sin implies a conversion, a fundamental disaffiliating oneself from the realities that are perceived as sinful. "Consciousness of evil, in fact, originates in the process of conversion itself."[2] We only define the present situation as sinful when we have created an alternative construct; when we have shifted paradigms. But one problem remains. After confessing guilt, there still remains the issue of making amends. Merely admitting the racism in our society does not result in distancing ourselves from that sin. We forget that we are, at best, "recovering racists." In the same way, for the bishops to merely admit that the church is awash in the sin of sexism leaves them "recovering sexists." The infection runs deep and is not easily healed.

So it is not enough for society, including the institutional church, to acknowledge sin in the past and in the present. In the words of the catechism, there must be "a firm purpose of amendment." Without that, conversion is superficial. The conversion spoken of here is not an intellectual or spiritual conversion but, as described by Pauli Murray, a conversion of one's whole life, entwining love of God and love of neighbor together so they become one. "Conversion to Christ, whose saving work is seen as radical liberation from all forms of enslavement and alienation, implies conversion to the neighbor."[3]

In speaking of sin, we speak of the "fundamental option" of people's lives; whether the basic orientation of life is toward God or away from God. Both individual sin and social sin are understood in the light of this fundamental option. Sinful societies and individuals are in constant need of renewing and reconciling so as not to obscure the face of God.

### Tension Between Virtue and Vice

Consciousness of systemic sin sometimes makes virtue of fault and fault of virtue. What is depicted as virtue or as evil in one system, takes on another color when the paradigm shifts. "Virtue," Anne E. Patrick asserts, "is a thoroughly social phenomenon, for groups of all types are distinguished by the traits and dispositions they foster in their members.... This involves acknowledging that an agent's social context determines to some degree the ideals of character he or she will develop."[4] Role models held up by the community, rewards bestowed and punishments inflicted, rituals and celebrations, myths and stories and traditions all serve to fit persons into their culture. At the same time, they reinforce the values of that culture. Traditional standards for a "good woman," a "saintly mother," or a "holy nun" describe too well the qualities of character that were and often are encouraged by the church and that many women strove to attain. In patriarchal cultures especially, the virtues exacted of women are different from those expected of men.

The standards for Christian sanctity are different for men and women; the roots of this distinction may be found in traditional Jewish customs regarding religious obligations.[5] Jewish men are called to develop a sensitivity to the religious dimensions of life by study and by observances such as participation in the *minyan*, praying the *Shema* daily, being called to read the Torah, but women are not enjoined to pray at specific times, they are not counted in the *minyan*, they are not required to study the Torah. The Talmud records that when Rabbi Hiya was asked what was the merit of women in the Torah, he replied: "Their merit arises from the fact that they take their children to their place of study and that they receive their husbands when they return home."[6] Women's virtue, then, lies in making it possible for their husbands and sons to fulfill the law.

The panegyric on the valiant woman (Prv 31:10–31), while raising the tasks of weaving, cooking, and household management to the heights of great virtue, set up different measures of goodness for women than for men. A privatized concept of goodness undergirds the poem, domesticating virtue and suggesting that nothing more is necessary for sanctity among women than caring for husbands and children. Sanctity is measured by service to one's husband and family. Important as that is, when it is the only consideration, women are excluded from all the public and political facets of life. Paul tells women to regard their husband as they regard the Lord, submitting to him as the church does to the Lord (Eph 5:22–24). In another place (Col 3:18–4:1), he speaks of the obedience of children, slaves, and wives. I will speak about obedience later.

Pope John Paul II's letter, *Mulieris Dignitatem*, reinforces women's secondary role and her call to a different sanctity than that of men. "When the author of the letter to the Ephesians calls Christ 'the bridegroom' and the church 'the bride,' he indirectly confirms through this analogy the truth about woman as bride. The bridegroom is one who loves. The bride is loved: It is she who receives love in order to love in return" (#29).

We have only to look at the calendar of saints for another illustration of the different set of standards by which women are measured. Virgin, widow, and martyr almost exhausts the catalogue of women saints; while men are king, soldier, priest, bishop, pope, farmer, confessor, doctor, and martyr, but certainly not virgins and widowers. Again, different norms for sanctity.[7] The canonization of Maria Goretti tragically illustrates the point: Better dead than sullied by being a victim of rape. "While Christians may explicitly condemn the act that brought about Maria's sainthood, her martyrdom teaches that suffering and the acts that caused the suffering are signs that she had been blessed. Thus sexual assault, particularly if the actual loss of virginity is avoided, can be a blessing in disguise."[8]

Feminism has altered the valuation of good and evil. Once-exalted virtues and once-condemned vices have been judged and have been found to ratify one form of evil even as they denounced another. The injunctions of Jesus against the proud and powerful when preached to the lowly and powerless do not bear the same message. In fact, they become oppressive. We have only to think of the scripture as preached to slaves calling for obedience and respect toward the master or as preached to women calling for submission to husbands. In this regard, Gustavo Gutierrez told a story about how poor peasants heard the parable about the landowner who sent his servants to collect the tax from the tenants (Mk 12). When the servants beat the tax collectors, the owner sent his son who was also killed. When the peasants heard this, they cheered. How could we expect them to have done otherwise?[9]

### In the Name of Obedience

One insidious aspect of systemic sin is that victims often cooperate with the forces of their oppression in the name of obedience. Dorothee Söelle questions the value of Christian obedience as we have known it. In the light of the Holocaust and the Nuremberg trials, she asks, "Is it possible that Christian training in obedience can be, even partially, responsible for the good conscience of a bureaucratic murderer?"[10] My Lai, Watergate, and the other public travesties of justice we have witnessed raise the same question. Has the church emphasized the virtue of obedience so much that it has neglected the virtue of a critical conscience? Are Christians more susceptible to cooperating with sinful structures because of an exalted sense of obedience?

The research of Stanley Milgram is a stark reminder of the power of obedience and of what Hannah Arendt called the banality of evil. Milgram devised an experiment at Yale University in which he measured how much pain ordinary persons were willing to inflict on another simply because they were ordered to do so. He discovered that most adults were willing to go to almost any lengths at the command of an authority figure. The participants: students, professionals, white and blue collar workers, and unemployed persons, were told that in order to study the effect of punishment on learning, they were to administer an electric shock for every wrong response given by the learner. The learner, who was part of the experimenting team, moaned, cried out, and screamed as participants pressed the button they thought increased the voltage. About sixty percent of the subjects administered what they believed to be dangerous and lethal electric shocks because the experimenter urged them on, ordered them to continue. When the authority figure was removed and the subjects told that they could administer whatever voltage they deemed appropriate to wrong answers, the average shock administered was less than sixty volts, lower than the point at which the "victim" indicated any sign of discomfort. Milgram reported,

> This is perhaps the most fundamental lesson of our study: ordinary people, simply doing their jobs, and without any particular hostility on their part, can become agents in a terrible destructive process. Moreover, even when the destructive effects of their work become patently clear, and they are asked to carry out actions incompatible with fundamental standards of morality, relatively few people have the resources needed to resist authority.[11]

Sheila Redmond has raised the specter of child abuse as one result of an overemphasis on obedience. Children are taught to respect and obey parents and other adults. In the child's mind, the adult is always right and what an adult asks must be right. Besides, if a child disobeys, the love of the adult may be lost. Redmond draws a connection between Jesus' willingness to obey even unto death with a child's belief that what the father does is justifiable and must be obeyed. After all, the salvation of the human race is thought to be effected by pedocide, the death of the Son to appease the Father. This religious symbolism tolerates and justifies family violence.

> If a child's priest, minister, or father abuses her or him, it is only natural that the abused child, who is raised in a Christian environment, find the blame within her or him-

self. Within the framework of patriarchal Christianity, the child is almost powerless to reject abuse. She cannot tell anyone just how evil she really is, and therefore is severely hampered in ever fully resolving the damage done by the assault through rejection of the internalized guilt.[12]

The obedience we owe is not unthinking compliance to authority, undiscriminating conformity to customs and laws, but rather critical analysis and mature responsibility in decision making. In complex societies, good order requires cooperation and a certain obedience to rules and laws. Imagine the chaos if we were to abandon the traffic laws, and people were free to decide on their own how fast to drive, when to yield or stop, or even where to park. What is needed is a balance between obedience to just laws and a critical analysis of laws in general, even those deemed just. Laws which demean human beings require the courage to disobey. The midwives Shiphrah and Puah, who ignored the law of Pharaoh and saved Moses and other Hebrew infant boys, and Lilith and Vashti are models of courageous disobeyers. In our own century, the Christians who hid Jews from the Nazis, the Civil Rights demonstrators, and the anti-Apartheid protesters of South Africa assumed the responsibility to challenge unjust laws by virtuous disobedience. Such courage is not taken lightly; the decision to accept the consequences of one's actions plays a major role in such public confrontations.

Not all disobedience is so dramatic and public. Women and other subordinate peoples are learning the virtue of disobedience and non-compliance with domination. Women are breaking the rules that govern the "good woman's" life. They are demanding to be involved in decisions that affect their lives and are not willing to merely adhere to regulations imposed from on high. Having taken their experience as women in society and in the church seriously, they are reluctant to live by guidelines that do not take their experiences seriously. The widespread non-compliance with the dictates of *Humanae Vitae* is but one indication of the willingness to disobey commands in which women's experience is not listened to and reverenced, but one indication of women's reliance on and obedience to their own conscience.

Disobedience is not altogether a new story. Founders of active religious congregations were forced to disobey the conventions of their day and the injunctions of popes and bishops in order to answer the call to minister to the sick and needy. Courageous disobedience is often costly. In the last century, Margaret Cusack, the founder of the Sisters of St. Joseph of Peace, was not submissive to bishops, disobeyed their injunctions, and was finally forced into a decision to abandon her congregation in order that it might survive. During her lifetime, in 1895, the Sacred Congregation approved her order but required that it efface all signs of Miss Cusack from community documents, drop the word "peace" from their title, and remove the cross and dove from their religious habit. Her memory and the word "peace" were not reclaimed until 1970.[13]

Even contemplative sisters are opting for the virtue of disobedience. In 1969 at Woodstock, Maryland, 135 cloistered sisters signed a letter of protest against *Venite Seorsum,* a decree issued by the Vatican which stated that those who opposed papal enclosure could develop some other kind of religious life but that they should leave the traditional form of papal cloister.[14] In each case, the sisters were responding to a different understanding of church, authority, revelation, and theology than representatives of the institutional church.

More recently, Agnes Mansour, Director of Social Services for the state of Michigan,[15] Arlene Violet, Attorney General of Rhode Island, and Elizabeth Morancy, member of the Rhode Island House of Representatives, all Sisters of Mercy, chose not to obey orders from bishops. In obeying their own consciences they were forced to leave their religious congregations. And yet free will and freedom of conscience are ideals that the church has always held sacred. The institutional church needs to maintain and respect an atmosphere of freedom that encourages the examination of traditional norms for today. This freedom would insure the right of a sincere conscience to doubt certain norms which may not be questioned by other sincere Christians. The gospel is not set in stone; it must be interpreted and reinterpreted in an ongoing manner. Feminist interpretations today are calling unthinking obedience and uncritical compliance into question.

### The Gift of Anger[16]

Obedience is not the only virtue/vice brought into question in the tension between individual sin and systemic sin. God has blessed us with the gift of anger so that our zeal and passion for justice may be enkindled. As one of the prophetic forces in our day, feminism and the attendant consciousness of the oppression of women often lead to anger—justified anger—but anger nonetheless: anger at society and at the church, when they remain blind to the ways in which they use and abuse women.

Beverly Harrison, in her inaugural lecture at Union Theological Seminary, insisted that "Anger is a mode of connectedness to others and it is always a vivid form of caring…the power of anger is the work of love."[17] Not to be angry in the face of injustice, not to be angry when confronted with violence, not to be angry in seeing the extent of hunger and homelessness, not to be angry at the exploitation and abuse of children, not to be angry at the number of battered women, is to be unloving.

Most of us react with varying degrees of anger to this litany of evil when others are victimized, but when a woman finds herself the victim, she often denies herself the right to express anger. She assumes responsibility for the violence in her life. Social workers and counselors who work with battered women report conversations like: "If I had the house clean, the kids quiet, the dinner ready, he would not hit me." "He's tired, frustrated, dejected, that's why he beats me." "If only I were prettier, more intelligent, younger…." Every woman's situation is not so dramatic, but many women are reluctant to allow themselves to be angry when they themselves are victimized. They have been socialized to discount their own welfare for the benefit of others, and they judge concern for themselves as selfishness. Often, then, justified anger erupts in inappropriate ways. "As with any repressed anger, the result is depression and sadness: loss of energy, of zest, of a taste for life, inability to pray or to relate in a trusting and loving way with anyone."[18] All of this, of course, leads to feelings of guilt and self-doubt.

Women have not had enough experience in facing and expressing anger. They have been taught that nice girls don't get mad. They have been encultured to take responsibility for the nurturing and maintenance of relationships and this has often been translated as "peace at any price." In order to maintain relationships, women have denied their anger or have turned it on themselves. Few women ever asked whether the relationship ought to be maintained or whether it ought to be transformed. Few women asked whether the price was too high, whether the peace was not peace at all but simply an absence of war.

Some women have also learned to deny their anger because they are so vulnerable to violence; they avoid situations that might unleash someone else's anger. We are left, then, with the widespread incidence of the battered woman's syndrome, women remaining in abusive situations because of the fear of what may befall them if they were in touch with righteous anger and took steps to escape the brutality in their lives.

At times, the virtue of anger demands rage on our part. Elizabeth Carroll, S.M., pioneer in the Catholic Women's movement, worried as she grew older that she might be losing her anger. "And then," she said, "I will be good for nothing." Rage is not the appropriate response to a tornado or an earthquake. Rage arises when alternatives are possible, when what exists ought not to be, and when conditions could be changed. Anger in the face of injustice and oppression is the virtuous response. Anger energizes and focuses attention. It is an expression of passionate care and concern in the face of evil.

Besides being a sign that evil in this world must be deplored, appropriate anger, virtuous anger, is also a signal that a person has developed self confidence and self respect and will not tolerate what ought not be tolerated. It is a sign that a person has matured enough to stand alone, if need be, for one's principles.

Inappropriate anger, anger exhibited in passive-aggressive behavior, irrational outbursts, and infantile attacks are familiar enough experiences to warrant social and religious prohibitions against anger. But social and religious prohibitions have sometimes been extended to include even the virtue of anger. Because we have not taken anger as a virtue seriously enough, we have not developed the resources to express it in positive, caring, and productive ways. Anger is both an emotion and a way of behaving. Cultural restrictions on women, the definition of the good woman, have left many women without the strength and courage to express legitimate anger. Harriet Lerner declares that:

> The expression of legitimate anger and protest is more than a statement of dignity and self-respect. It is also a statement that one will risk standing alone, even in the face of disapproval or the potential loss of love from others.... Not only have women been taught that their value, if not their very identity, rests largely on their loving and being loved, but also, even more to the point, many women have not achieved the degree of autonomous functioning that would permit them to stand separate and alone in the experience of their anger.[19]

When anger is a healthy response to the violation of herself, a woman may draw on the energy of that anger to reclaim herself and to develop her ability for intimacy. In the process, she will mourn the diminishment of herself and of her relationships that her anger revealed.

Let me make myself clear. Anger may be destructive; it may lead to violence and abuse of others or ourselves. But it is not anger itself that is the problem; rather, the underlying problem is a fear and avoidance of all strong emotions. Instead of learning to feel the full range of our emotions and to allow them to nurture us and others, we deny them as if they are wrong, we repress them until they exert themselves in sometimes harmful ways. We have been intent on developing the human mind and the human body, but we are still ignorant of how to develop the human emotions. God has blessed us with the gift of anger in order that our zeal may be enkindled and our passion for justice aroused.

### The Place of Pride

The third virtue/vice I will consider is pride, which we find at the head of the list of the seven capital sins, those evils that give rise to all others. The myth of the fall of Adam identifies two prominent faces of sin, sensuality and pride. As a result of the Genesis story, Eve (and all women with her) has been assigned the character of seductress and temptress. The traditional interpretation of the Genesis account also teaches that the first sin was (and is) pride and arrogance in the face of God. The serpent had promised, after all, that "You will be like gods, knowing good and evil" (Gn 3:5). Indeed, this notion is so strong that Reinhold Niebuhr held that "Biblical and Christian tradition has maintained with a fair degree of consistency that pride is more basic than sensuality and that the latter is, in some way, derived from the former."[20] Pride, in this sense, is an unjustified concern for one's power and prestige; it is characterized by aggressiveness, exploitation, and self aggrandizement. These are precisely the mechanisms for survival in a hierarchical and patriarchal culture. They are attempts to overcome the fears and uncertainties about surviving in a competitive and aggressive society.

More than thirty years ago, Valerie Saiving's seminal essay "The Human Situation: A Feminine Viewpoint" challenged whether sin as traditionally defined adequately described women's situation. Traditional theology, written by men who were caught up in the tensions of a hypermasculine culture, identifies sin with pride, the desire for power, aggression, self-assertiveness, and exploitation. These qualities identify the context of most men's lives. But they are not the context of most women's existence. Women, according to Saiving, were more likely to be involved in sins of triviality, in the lack of an organizing center to their lives, in defining themselves in terms of another, in mistrusting reason in favor of emotions, and in general in an underdevelopment of the self.[21]

Jürgen Moltmann contends that humanity's wanting to be like God is only one side of sin; despair, hopelessness, inertia, and melancholy the other. "Temptation consists not so much in the titanic desire to be like God, but in weakness, timidity, weariness, not wanting to be what God requires of us."[22]

Theologically, underdevelopment of one's humanity is identified as sin. That is not the language of psychology but the issue is of major concern to psychologists. Notable work by psychologists such as Jean Baker Miller claim that in our society we force men to center around themselves and women to center around others. Miller calls for a social revolution that identifies service to others not in terms of subservience but in terms of mutuality. It is a revolution that would encourage men to fully integrate concern for others with concern for self and socialize women to have the right to act and judge in terms of direct benefits to themselves.[23]

Many women are infected with what has been called the good-girl syndrome. They need no outside restrictions: no chaperone, no protector, no convent walls, no bound feet, no veils, no harem. Women interiorize society's expectations, and they monitor themselves. They become their own internal police force. They have interiorized society's image of the perfect woman as subordinate, genteel, respectable, and above suspicion. Young women are still encultured to please. They are still encouraged to define themselves by how they look, how they dress, how they walk and sit and talk. They smile more than men, they agree more readily, they hide their own successes and praise those of men. Above all else, they aim to please, but in the process, they are minimized in their own eyes and in the eyes of others.

Each year I ask my undergraduate students to survey their young women friends to see how many have ever lied to a male friend when her grades were better than his. Invariably, they find bright young women who deny their own success. Sometimes, the response is that women also lie about their grades when they are better than their female friends. Women do no yet know how to handle success. Matina Horner's study that unearthed a "fear of success syndrome" among college-age women is not simply an historical analysis, a record of another time. It is relevant today. Georgia Sassen[24] and others extended that study and suggest that perhaps women know the cost of success in this society and prefer not to pay the price. In either case, women are left with unresolved negative feelings. Denying one's successes is not only a bogus humility, it also suggests something negative about one's associates. Is the male ego so fragile that it cannot stand to have a woman flourish? Are female friends so vulnerable that they cannot rejoice in the accomplishments of another woman? The "good girl" not only has not had enough practice in appropriately expressing anger, she has not had enough practice in celebrating her own gifts and talents. In fact, her behavior is that of a "healthy feminine woman" without rancor. Harriet Lerner maintains that "girls are raised in a manner that restricts their freedom to express anger and aggression and inhibits their capacity for competitive and self-assertive behavior, as well."[25]

Judith Plaskow, in *Sex, Sin and Grace,* rejected not only Niebuhr's claim that pride is the cardinal or root sin, she also rejected his suggestion that grace consisted in the shattering of the prideful self. "The shattering of the self from beyond is received as grace only where the self's sin is pride and self-absorption. Where sin is not 'too much self' but the lack of self, such shattering is at least irrelevant and possibly destructive rather than healing.... Where sin is not the attempt to take everything on the self, but the failure to take responsibility, the failure to become a self, pardon addressed to the prideful self has less meaning."[26]

Changing the concept of sin forces a change in the concept of grace. For subordinate and dominated peoples, grace comes in the form of affirmation, respect, and the development of a healthy and holy pride in oneself, not in crucifying the prideful self but in the resurrection of a redeemed self into new life.

### Tension Between Law and Relationship
It would be as unfair and untrue for feminists to categorize traditional ethical principles as legalistic and feminist ethical principles as caring, as it is for Christians to categorize Judaism as a religion of law and Christianity as a religion of love. We forget that what Jesus knew about love he learned from his Jewish parents in a Jewish community. His teachings are rooted in the Hebrew scriptures. On the other hand, even a cursory look at Christian history reveals injustice, vengeance, and violence carried out in the name of the law; worse still, in the name of love.

The basis of all just laws and of an ethic of caring is the dignity of the human person. Laws are meant to safeguard that dignity for individuals and for society as a whole. Laws, rules, and commandments are ordinarily composed in order to make life together in the human community possible. For the most part, it is not the law that is at fault but the rigid adherence to the law as law. Laws need to be revised and reinterpreted according to the needs and insights of different times and places. Just laws are meant to and do protect us, but our obligation is to measure and weigh laws so that we do not presume justice prematurely. Divorced from human relationships, concerns, and responsibilities, the law can kill. Adherence to the law without concern for the lives of women and men is an irreligious act; compliance with unjust laws is a sinful one. Describing this from a Jewish perspective, Judith Plaskow contends that the law has its religious origins in the passion for relation. But when it takes on a life of its own, apart from relationship, it may be a barrier between persons and between humanity and God. Observance of the law then becomes a substitute for the very relation it was meant to defend and protect, and "God's law" replaces God in a self-perpetuating system.[27] Then the distinction between legality and morality is blurred. The language of laws and rules and commandments determines morality. It is as if civil or ecclesial legality guarantees morality. This presumption of morality for what is only legal results from an unformed and uninformed conscience.

The dignity of the human person, the basis of both law and of love, is manifested and protected by concern for individual freedom and a concern for relationships. Human freedom is neither absolute nor perfect. We are all relatively free in a limited way to decide what kind of a person we are and will become. Family, society, church, and governments limit freedom. Education, finances, talents, and intelligence, or lack thereof, limit freedom. The weather and the level of our energy limit freedom. Relationships, all of them, limit freedom. Even relationships that foster and encourage freedom limit freedom for the benefit of the relationship itself. Human dignity is best honored in the balance between freedom and relationship.

Some theologians are focusing attention more on the relationships than on the law in their discussions of morality. They are introducing alternative methodologies and theories into the conversation. Goodness and evil, virtue and vice are judged primarily by their impact on relationships with God, with others, and with self. Sin is not so much breaking the law of God as putting one's relationship with God into jeopardy. The very idea of sin is based on the foundational notion that how we act with one another, what we do to and with other human beings affects God. Our God is a relational God, and we have been created to be in relation with God. Sin is a distortion of that relationship. Sin also distorts relationships between human beings; it even infects the relationship with oneself.

Being relational creatures and belonging to the human community, women and men are responsible for that community and its relationships even as they are free to determine their own destiny. "They are not, then, merely to be used by others, exploited, choked off in their freedom."[28] Nor are they absolutely free to determine their destiny without any consideration of the consequences to others. "And because they are the kind of beings that can love God with all their heart and mind and strength, and their neighbor even as themselves, they are not to be denied participation in human community, they are not to be isolated as pure freedoms to which we can be indifferent so long as we do not interfere in their lives."[29]

We are called to freedom in community. But this presupposes that the community is one that supports and nurtures human life. It is impossible to be free, self determining, in a society that restricts growth and development by rule, by custom, or by tradition. When certain areas of human development are closed off to some people, all of society is poorer. Lack of respect, education, shelter, food, and health care lessens the freedom of the poor and ultimately of all of society. Unfortunately, we are learning from sad experience that adults who were battered as children are more likely to become batterers themselves. We have also discovered that the learned violence and hatred that turned young men into soldiers is not easily forgotten after the conflict. We can only speculate how homelessness is scarring thousands of children, denying them freedom, and restricting their development.

The relational and communal aspect of sin is addressed by theologians as dissimilar as Mary Daly and Rosemary Radford Ruether. In one of her earlier works, *Beyond God the Father*,[30] Daly speaks of sin as false naming in which the male viewpoint is metamorphosed into God's viewpoint. Evil and responsibility for evil are imposed upon women, and the cosmic misnaming of women results in the misnaming of men and of God. This false naming manifests itself in two ways: in the patriarchal stealing of women's power to name themselves and in women's accepting being named or defined by another. In a later work, Daly reclaims the word "sin" which is etymologically related to the Latin *est* (he/she is). Its root is derived from the Indo-European root *es* meaning 'to be.' "Clearly, our ontological courage, our courage to be, implies the courage to be wrong. Elemental be-ing is Sinning; it requires the Courage to Sin."[31] It requires the courage to be wrong according to the false naming and to be right in freely naming oneself.

Ruether expresses it differently. "Sexism as sin centers on distorted relationality."[32] In a hierarchical society, the self-other duality is confused with the good-evil duality that identifies the dominant group as the human norm and the others as inferior, thus providing the rationalization for exploitation. As a result of the exploitation, the suppressed group internalizes the dominant ideology and is socialized into behaviors and attitudes that perpetuate the oppression. One of the earliest distortions of the self-other relationship is the perversion of humanity as male and female into a relationship of superiority and inferiority. Relationships in which one partner has not developed an authentic self can never become I-Thou relationships in which human subject meets human subject. Relationality demands freedom.

The relational dimension of human dignity suggests that decisions need to be made in such a way that the good of the community is taken into consideration. This ability to make moral decisions taking "the good of the community" into account has been investigated under two very different rubrics by Lawrence Kohlberg and Carol Gilligan. Kohlberg used the perspective of justice, Gilligan that of care, in examining how persons make moral decisions. In both experiments, dilemmas were presented in such a way that non-violent solutions were precluded. Each decision involved choosing one evil rather than another. What both psychologists measured was the motivation behind the

choices people made, not the choice itself. Their schemes regarding moral development do not take into account whether or
not a person would choose to steal or have an abortion or not.
They are only concerned with motivation.

In Kohlberg's work, the relational bias in women's thinking
was interpreted negatively as a low level moral decision-making
mechanism. But as Gilligan describes women's ways of moral
judgment, the language of care and non-violence, she offers another perspective. She describes a moral development in women
that moves from a position of selfishness to one of self-sacrifice
and finally to responsibility for care; a care that includes both
self and others and which opts for the solution that appears to
offer the least violence.

Gilligan's change in focus from justice to care leads to alternative insights about what is or is not moral. She maintains
that the dilemma is the same for both sexes:

> ...a conflict between integrity and care. But approached
> from different perspectives, this dilemma generates the rec-
> ognition of opposite truths.... The morality of rights is pred-
> icated on equality and centered on fairness, while the ethic
> of responsibility relies on the concept of equality, the rec-
> ognition of differences in need. While the ethic of rights is a
> manifestation of equal respect, balancing the claims of the
> other and self, the ethic of responsibility rests on an under-
> standing that gives rise to compassion and care.[33]

The experiments indicate that, on an average, women emphasize care in making moral decisions, and men emphasize justice. For men, the moral imperative manifests itself as respect
and protection for the rights of others; for women, it is revealed
in a responsibility to care for and alleviate the troubles of the
world. Men might, for example, describe the inequities in society
as injustice while women might describe the same situation in
terms of violence. The one premise calls for equality, the other
for a minimizing of hurt. It is not that one or the other makes a
case for evil. One does not necessarily negate the other. Concern
for either care or justice to the detriment of the other, is the effect

of socialization into a society that maintains different roles and character qualities for each of the sexes. In a less rigidly gender-determined culture, both care and justice might be elements of the decision-making process of both men and women.

The three tensions I have discussed here—between individual and societal responsibility for sin, between identifying behaviors as virtue or vice, and between a legal and relational concept of evil, do not deny the existence of sin. Rather, they oblige us to assume more responsibility for sin that saturates the world and to acknowledge our culpability for the condition of the world. That acknowledgment makes it more difficult to blame God for what has been done by humanity. It also makes it more difficult to simply pray that God will care for tomorrow. It forces us to acknowledge, at least implicitly, that we are either cooperating with the Spirit in creating the future or we are creating a future that will have little to do with the reign of God.

### Questions for Reflection

1. How has your idea of sin changed since you were an adolescent? In what ways has it changed?

2. What is your reaction to the possibility that anger, pride, and disobedience are sometimes virtuous? How can a person be sure that they are virtues and not vices in a particular setting?

3. What is the connection between individual responsibility and systemic sin?

4. In your opinion, how are most moral decisions made, for the good of individuals or for the good of the community?

### Endnotes

1. Anne E. Patrick, "Power and Responsibility: Changing Paradigms of Virtue," Georgetown University, January 18, 1990. Lecture notes.

2. Rosemary Radford Ruether, *Sexism and God-Talk: Toward a Feminist Theology* (Boston: Beacon Press, 1983) 59.

3. Pauli Murray, "Black Theology and Feminist Theology: A Comparative View" *Anglican Theological Review* LX: 1 (January 1978) 7.

4. Anne E. Patrick, "Power and Responsibility," 3-4.

5. For feminist developments in Jewish thought, see Rabbi Sally Priesand, *Judaism and the New Woman* (New York: Behrman House, 1975); Elizabeth Kolton, *The Jewish Woman* (New York: Schocken Books, 1976); Roslyn Lacks, *Women and Judaism* (Garden City, N.Y.: Doubleday,

1980); Susannah Heschel, ed. *On Being a Jewish Feminist: A Reader* (New York: Schocken, 1983), and Judith Plaskow, *Standing Again at Sinai: Judaism from a Feminist Perspective* (San Francisco: Harper & Row, 1990).

6. Ann Goldfield, "Women as Sources of Torah in the Rabbinic Tradition," in *The Jewish Woman*, 258.

7. Two women have been declared Doctors of the Church in this century: Teresa of Avila and Catherine of Siena. The delayed honor proves the point.

8. Sheila Redmond, "Christian 'Virtues' and Recovery from Child Sexual Abuse" in *Christianity, Patriarchy and Abuse* edited by Joanne Carlson Brown and Carole R. Bohn (New York: Pilgrim Press, 1989) 75.

9. Lecture, Boston college, 1979.

10. Dorothee Söelle, *Beyond Mere Obedience* (New York: The Pilgrim Press, 1982) 9.

11. Stanley Milgram, "The Perils of Obedience," *Harper's Magazine*, December 1973, 75-76.

12. Sheila A. Redmond, "Christian 'Virtues' and Recovery from Child Abuse" in *Christianity, Patriarchy and Abuse*: edited by Joanne Carlson Brown and Carole R. Bohn, 78-79. Citation, 79.

13. See Dorothy Vidulich, *Peace Pays a Price* (Teaneck, NJ: Garden State Press, 1975).

14. Mary Jo Weaver, *New Catholic Women: A Contemporary Challenge to Traditional Religious Authority* (San Francisco: Harper and Row, 1985) 101-102.

15. See Madonna Kolbenschlag, ed. *Authority, Community and Conflict* (Kansas City: Sheed and Ward, 1986) for a full discussion of the conflict regarding Agnes Mansour.

16. See Beverly Harrison, "The Power of Anger in the Work of Love," *Union Theological Seminary Quarterly* 36 Supplementary, 1981; Carolyn Osiek, R.S.C.J., *Beyond Anger: On Being a Feminist in the Church* (New York: Paulist Press, 1986); Harriet G. Lerner, *The Dance of Anger* (New York: Harper & Row, 1985); James and Evelyn Whitehead, Chapter 9, "Anger and Forgiveness," *Seasons of Strength* (Garden City, N.Y.: Doubleday, 1984).

17. Beverly Harrison, "The Power of Anger," 49.

18. Carolyn Osiek, *Beyond Anger*, 13.

19. Harriet E. Lerner, "Internal Prohibitions Against Anger," *The American Journal of Psychoanalysis* 40:2 (1980).

20. Reinhold Niebuhr, *The Nature and Destiny of Man* (New York: Charles Scribner's Sons, 1964) 186.

21. Valerie Saiving, "The Human Situation: A Feminine View," *The Journal of Religion* (April 1960).

22. Jurgen Moltmann, *Theology of Hope* (New York: Harper & Row, 1962) 22-23.

23. Jean Baker Miller, *Toward a New Psychology of Women* (Boston: Beacon Press, 1976) 68-73.

24. Georgia Sassen, "Success Anxiety in Women: A Constructivist

Interpretation of its Source and its Significance" *Harvard Educational Review* 50:1 (February 1980).

25. Lerner, "Internal Prohibitions" 138.

26. Judith Plaskow, *Sex, Sin and Grace: Women's Experience and the Theologies of Reinhold Niebuhr and Paul Tillich* (Washington: University of America Press, 1980) 85-86.

27. Judith Plaskow, *Standing Again at Sinai: Judaism from a Jewish Perspective* (San Francisco: Harper & Row, 1990) 69.

28. Margaret A. Farley, "From Moral Insight to Moral Choice: Discernment and Decision-Making in the Christian Community" Meeting of the Leadership Conference of Women Religious, New Orleans, 1985. Notes 1-2.

29. Ibid., 2.

30. Mary Daly, *Beyond God the Father: Toward a Philosophy of Women's Liberation* (Boston: Beacon Press, 1973), 47.

31. Mary Daly, *Pure Lust: Elemental Feminist Philosophy* (Boston: Beacon Press, 1984), 151.

32. Rosemary Radford Ruether, *Sexism and God-Talk*, 174.

33. Carol Gilligan, *In a Different Voice* (Cambridge: Harvard University Press, 1982) 164-165.

# 7

# Women in
# the Hebrew Scriptures

As the ceiling of the Sistine Chapel was cleaned of the centuries of grime and soot, new colors, tones, and shadings appeared that startled the art world. The brilliant colors: scarlets, mint greens, deep reds, royal blues, surprised everyone because Michelangelo was not known as a great colorist. The job is tedious; care must be taken so that only the accumulation of the ages is removed and nothing of the painting itself. Inch by inch, artists painstakingly and with great delicacy daub away at the dirt, leaving the original as untouched as possible. As can be expected, there was great controversy about whether the job should be done at all.

James Beck, head of Columbia University's art department, insists that "the bright new colors are incorrect. They were made to have a filtered layer. That layering, I maintain, has been removed."[1] Other art experts "rejoice that Michelangelo has been restored to us, as he was known to his contemporaries; a great colorist and a great sculptor."[2]

---

The Sistine ceiling is a good analogy for what is happening in theology today, particularly among biblical scholars. The scriptures are being subjected to the technology and knowledge of the twentieth century so that the original may be perceived more clearly. As with the Sistine restoration, there is controversy. Shouldn't we just accept what has been handed down? What if some of the original work is misread or destroyed? Aren't the accretions of the centuries now part of the story? On the one side are those who understand recent biblical scholarship as "destroying tradition." On the other side are those who understand it as restoring the tradition. Feminist biblical scholars are among the restorers, and though they are not the only ones, they are making dramatic and significant contributions. They are, like the artists, trying to remove non-essential accumulations in order to understand the original more faithfully. It is not a work that is done lightly.

Biblical scholars, of course, are not just trying to see through centuries of accretions, and not just trying to understand the original political, economic, social, and cultural aspects of the biblical author's worldview. They are also trying to read the scriptures in the light of twentieth-century insights. In the process, they have come to understand that each age interprets the good news according to its own lights and it is the responsibility of each age to discover how it may interact with the bible so that it may truly be the living word of God.

### Two Cautions

The first caution in undertaking a study of feminist interpretation of scripture (or for that matter, any interpretation of scripture) is: Do not *underrate* scripture. The authors of the bible lived in a patriarchal society in which women were considered the property of their fathers or husbands. The scriptures, therefore, have an undeniable androcentric tone; the male is the center of attention and action. Most of the images and metaphors are masculine, the history recorded is the account of men's exploits, as reported by men to be read by men. Because of the misogynist attitude evident in many pages of scripture, there are feminists who regard the bible as irredeemably sexist and therefore not able to speak to women's experience. They believe that patriarchy, Judaism, and Christianity are so intimately involved with one another that there is no way to separate them; they constitute one another. Such a stand rejects the very basis of Jewish and Christian faith. It also denies the possibility that alternative interpretations may be made or that anything positive may be found. "There is a kind of apocalyptic finalism, rigid and unbending, which cannot yield to a dynamic of conversion."[3]

The second caution in reading scripture is not to *overrate* it. At the opposite end of the spectrum are women and men who look to the bible to find the final answer to all their concerns. It is as though all truth resided in the bible. They might look to Paul to understand the relationship between husbands and wives or they may construe the parables of Jesus in a literalist way. We simply cannot find all the answers in a book written by men who could not have imagined the complexity of life today. The men who wrote the bible could not escape their century, even as we cannot escape ours. Their culture, social standing, and education affected their writing, just as our culture, social standing, and education affect our reading. Scripture provides a kind of parameter, a fence, if you will, that indicates an area where the Christian solution to the questions of life may be found. Within that area we will find some conflicting issues, some that seem alien because they are culture-bound to the time and place of their writing, and some that support behavior we find reprehensible. But we will also find the core truths upon which our faith depends.

We speak of the bible as the living word of God. It is not the printed word that is alive. It is not the book itself that lives. Studying the bible as literature and critiquing its literary style are not dealing with the living word of God. The scriptures are the living word of God in relationship to the community that reads, reflects, and prays over its teachings. It lives in us or it does not live at all. Each generation is responsible to interact with the word, not to unthinkingly swallow it whole but to think, to reason, to know it "by heart." Scripture scholars use their knowledge of the languages, culture, history, and literature of the biblical era in their discipline. They use historical or literary or form criticism; they compare the books with one another and with other contemporary works. The Christian community is ordinarily not involved in this kind of study, much as we benefit from it. Our approach is best described as one of intimacy rather than mastery. "By intimacy here we do not mean a mystical or nonintellectual approach. Rather a *more-than* intellectual grasp of scripture is envisioned, a grasp that is informed by serious academic study but which 'knows from the inside.'"[4] The Christian community reads the bible from the viewpoint of faith, but always guided by the scholarship of biblical scholars.

This is not to suggest that biblical experts have stumbled upon the truth or are in agreement about how to interpret the scriptures. They may provide profound insights or they may not. We do well to be advised, informed, and educated by their learning. Part of our responsibility is to decide who it is that we should listen to; who appears to have interpreted the sacred word in a way that authentically reveals God to us.

> The challenge presented to those of us who seek the Reign of God in every age is to hear the biblical words as "focal instance." They are not the detailed blueprint for human society, nor will they be measured by the passing ideological agenda.... The Reign of God is experienced among those who are able to see in their own contexts how to act out of a vision schooled by the biblical stories.[5]

I sometimes wish I could read the bible for the first time. We carry with us so many childhood memories, so many images from homilies and lectures, so many stained-glass window portraits, that it is sometimes difficult to allow the words to come alive in a new and fresh way. We have to get rid of some baggage from sentimental or pious books of another era and bring the scriptures and our experience in conversation. This is not a new idea; all scripture is the result of experience, all of it has been read through the lens of each century's experience. Conjure up an image of the exodus, for example. Did your imagination place Miriam in a prominent place? Or did your memory flash back to a traditional rendition of Moses and perhaps Aaron lead-

ing a band of male Jews across the parted waters? We have not
seen enough images of Miriam leading the people in songs and
dances of praise to the Lord (Ex 15:20–21), or we have not been
reminded that the Lord spoke through Moses, Aaron, and
Miriam (Nm 12:4). Of course, we probably do know that she
was more severely punished than Aaron when they both criticized Moses (Nm 12). The old holy card picture illustrations,
like the written word, focus on the exploits of men, and that picture is still working in our imagination.

### Feminist Interpretations of Scripture[6]

The use of the adjective "feminist" here suggests that the interpretations do not claim to be neutral or value-free. Feminist
scholars take an advocacy stand for women. They ascribe significance to historical data as it oppresses or liberates women
and acknowledge that they are viewing the past through the particular lens of feminist theories. What is to be noted here is that
all interpretations of scripture are through a particular cultural
and historical lens: African, Asian, Latin American, American
Black, white male. There is no such thing as a value-free, neutral,
and objective reading of history, philosophy, science, or of scripture. The intellectually honest thing to do is to acknowledge that
and understand that our particular reading needs to be in dialogue with other readings. The specific questions, concerns, insights, and perspectives of Blacks, Hispanics, Asians, males, and
females are different, and each chooses from the scripture, perhaps unconsciously, those elements that help to link biblical
times with their lives in the here and now. For example, the exodus story was a profound metaphor for American slaves in the
last century, even as it is for Latin American theologians today.
In order to have a fuller understanding of scripture, we need to
be alert to both the positive and negative contributions that result from the various mind-sets of biblical scholars. None of us
has a hold on the truth.

Because the traditional readings of the bible have been
through the eyes of well-educated, middle-class, white males,
and because that has been the dominant ethos in our culture, we
sometimes think that their way is the only right way. When I

teach feminist theology, I try to keep a map of the world in the classroom. In making this point, I cover Europe with the palm of my hand and ask if we can believe in a God who chose to speak only through the theologians and hierarchy of that small area. Keeping a map or globe in sight helps to set studies in a larger context and prevent a myopic worldview.

This discussion is not concerned with those feminists who find the bible irredeemably sexist and who therefore reject it. Nor is it concerned with those feminists who read the scriptures in a literalist way. We will discuss feminist scholars (women and men) who believe that the bible is the word of God and who also recognize that it is deeply affected by the culture in which it was written and by the cultures of the interpreters through the ages. Interpreting the scriptures is not an exercise in proof texting (finding a quotation to support our own views). There is enough written to support almost any view.

Scripture was written over a period of more than a thousand years and indicates the values of the different periods of history. It reflects the social patterns and cultural influences of semi-nomadic peoples, of settled peasants, and of city dwellers, as well as the political views of a wide variety of people. We may get some insights into the life and culture, the values and aspirations of the various biblical periods, but we can not uncritically accept all those values or aspirations. The bible has been used to support war, slavery, and the subordination of women. Two prominent theologians, Rosemary Radford Ruether and Elisabeth Schüssler Fiorenza, have suggested guidelines for our reading of scripture through the lens of feminism.

### Prophetic Principle

According to Ruether, the prophetic principle arises from four themes of the liberating tradition of scripture: 1) God sides with the oppressed; 2) dominant systems of power and powerholders are critiqued; 3) the vision of the coming Reign of God, and 4) the critique of ideologies including religion (ideology is primarily religious in the bible).[7] Ruether's significant contribution in focusing on the prophetic principle is that it be turned back on itself. The bible is to be measured by its own words. What denies or invalidates the prophetic principle is not to be considered the word of God. Can we reply "This is the word of the Lord" when we hear this psalm: "May [the wicked and deceitful man's] days be few; may another seize his goods! May his children be fatherless, and his wife a widow! May his children wander about and beg; may they be driven out of the ruins they inhabit" (Ps 109). Or how do we react when we read: "Slaves, obey in everything those who are your earthly masters..." (Col 3:22)? Patriarchy, when measured in light of the four biblical themes, also falls under indictment. What is operating here is the principle of "ethical interiority," used from the beginning when it was decided that certain ritual laws and customs did not apply to the Christian community. As Ruether says, "Thus all theologies, regardless of their claims that the bible is totally the work of inspiration, in fact never consider all parts of the bible equally authoritative; rather they use texts according to implicit or explicit assumptions about the normative development of biblical faith."[8]

### Hermeneutics of Suspicion

Elisabeth Schüssler Fiorenza does not believe that there is one overarching principle, such as the prophetic principle, usable for feminists. We are able to find some liberating models in the bible but it is not because there is a correlation between feminist and biblical critical principles. Rather, women's experience enables us to discover them. Fiorenza, as mentioned earlier, has popularized the phrase "hermeneutics of suspicion" which "places a warning label on all biblical texts: 'Caution! Could be dangerous to your health and survival.'"[9]

The bible was written by men in androcentric language that makes women invisible. The language was selected and interpreted by men who lived in a male-centered society, often in a celibate male-centered society.

The first and never-ending task of a hermeneutics of suspicion, therefore, is to elaborate as much as possible the patriarchal, destructive aspects and oppressive elements of the bible.... We have to use a hermeneutics of suspicion to detect the antipatriarchal elements and functions of biblical texts, which are obscured and made invisible by androcentric language and concepts.[10]

The hermeneutics of suspicion calls for critical reading in order to discover the effect of patriarchy both on the author's history, song, myth, or parable, and also on the interpretation of scripture down the ages. But it also calls for critical reading in order to reveal liberating components. We search for hidden clues, for alternative interpretations, for insights which may uncover the liberating message of scripture for women and for men. Katie Geneva Cannon depicts how both the destructive and liberating message of scripture affected Black slaves. One the one hand, "Confidence in an omnipotent, omnipresent, and omniscient God helped slaves accommodate to the system of chattel slavery. With justice denied, hopes thwarted, and dreams shattered, Black Christians cited passages from the bible that gave them emotional poise and balance in the midst of their oppression." On the other hand, "The biblical interpretation of the Black church also made the slaves discontent with their servile condition.... The Black religious experience equipped slaves with a biblical understanding that called them to engage in acts of rebellion for freedom."[11]

Let us now turn our attention to some of the recent works of feminist biblical scholars. We will lift up both destructive and constructive depictions and considerations concerning women. Both are necessary if we are to reclaim scripture as truly liberating for women. It is not possible to read scripture in a feminist mode and disregard the sexism and misogyny with which it is laced. The main focus of the following section will be on reclaiming women who have been ignored, forgotten, or maligned; the bible stories will be read from a perspective different than the traditional one in order to provide an alternative understanding. Women's experience acts here as a filter through which the bible is understood and as the criterion for interpretation.

### Misogyny in the Bible

We have only to read the ten commandments to get some inkling about the condition of women in early Israel. There is no commandment "Thou shalt not rape," because rape was not considered a sin against women but rather a sin against the man who owned the woman, her master, father, or husband, and as such was covered under the command "You shall not covet your neighbor's house; you shall not covet your neighbor's wife, or his manservant, or his maidservant, or his ox, or his ass, or anything that is your neighbor's" (Ex 20:17).

Most of the laws of Israel are addressed to men who were responsible for their whole household. The woman's primary responsibility was to respect and obey her husband. She was valuable as the mother of sons. Since daughters left the family home upon marriage, sons could be counted on to carry on the inheritance and name. In the absence of sons, daughters were sometimes permitted to inherit (Nm 27:1–11).

Women in Israel were ritually unclean at the time of their menses and after sexual intercourse and childbirth (Lv 12 and 15). One indication of the attitude about women is that uncleanness lasted for seven days after the birth of a son but fourteen days after the birth of a daughter (Lv 12:1–5). Men also became ritually unclean after intercourse. Bodily emissions of all types rendered both women and men impure and excluded from participation in the religious practices of the community. The blood taboo is an ancient one that still affects us today. It is, in part, responsible for the argument against the ordination of women.

Divorce was a male privilege. The failure to produce a son was reason enough for divorce. In early Israel, women gave their slaves to their husbands in order to produce a male who would be counted as the son, not of the slave woman, but of the wife (Sarai, Rachel). Or the man simply took another wife. But in later biblical times divorce seemed to be the more common solution to the problem of the barren wife.

Many of the women we will discuss in this chapter have been negatively depicted and have been portrayed as models of passivity, weakness, deceit, and sin. They have been defined by patriarchy, and their words and actions have been judged only as they affected men's lives. Women in scripture are ordinarily noteworthy because of their relationship to a male hero.

Mothers, wives, and harlots play important roles but always subordinate to men. Traditionally, women have not been seen as central to the history of Israel or of the Christian foundations. These same women, seen through another lens, are recognized as significant in their own lives, contributing to the life and work of Israel, of Jesus, and of the early church.

### Reclaiming Eve[12]

Eve, Mother of all the Living, has been vilified down the ages because she seduced Adam into sin. It was she of whom Tertullian wrote, "You are the Devil's gateway.... You are the first deserter of the divine law.... You are she who persuaded him whom the Devil was not valiant enough to attack.... You destroyed so easily God's image man."[13] The story of the creation and fall of humanity has been used to support women's subordinate roles. Eve, who was only created to help Adam, has been held responsible for introducing sin into the world. The patriarchal pattern of the subjection of women to men was authorized by such teachings. Women were seen as essentially seductive, luring men into sin. The creation myth is also responsible for some attitudes common until recent times that women deserved to suffer in childbirth because God had so cursed them through Eve.

Phyllis Trible has provided an alternative reading that disallows male domination over women but also human domination over nature. She uses a literary approach, concentrating on the text itself rather than on other information such as archeological data, social or political setting, and historical background. She locates the text within a genre: legend, myth, folktale, letter, hymn, love song, etc. We do not, after all, read fairy tales the same way we read the editorial page of the daily paper. Trible looks for the meaning of the text by using the tool of rhetorical criticism, which investigates the distinct characteristics of the text in question. "The kinds of words used and the ways they are put together make every unit a new creation. In great variety, language plays with imagery, sounds, style, and viewpoints to yield particular distinctions, subtleties, and nuances."[14] The following is but a small taste of the exciting proposals Trible makes.

There are two creation stories; in Genesis 1, the account is of the seven days of creation with humanity created last. Chapter two, which interests us here, gives another version of creation. The Lord God had made earth and the heavens but the earth is barren and there is no creature to care for it. In just four verses, from 2:4 to 2:7 the word "earth" (*hā-ᵃdāmâ*) appears seven times, and the word for the creature (*hā-ᵃdām*) appears three times. The beginning of the story appears to emphasize the relationship of the first creature with the earth from which it was made. "Only two ingredients constitute its life, and both are tenuous: dusty earth and divine breath.... Combined by Yahweh, these fragile ingredients unite to form the creature who is totally dependent upon God."[15] The creature is still sexually undifferentiated. Upon realizing that the earth creature needs a companion like to itself, God decides to create a companion, an *ᵉzer* (a word used often to describe God). God puts the creature to sleep and from the one flesh, makes two, thereby creating human sexuality. "This divine act will alter radically the nature of *hā-ᵃdām* and bring about new creatures so that female and male together become one flesh that together is wholeness rather than isolation."[16] After this creation of sexuality, *hā-ᵃdām* speaks for the first time: "This, finally is bone of my bones and flesh of my flesh; this shall be called woman (*îššâ*) because from (*îš*) was this taken." This is another play on words that is not recognizable in translation.

If the creation story has been a weapon against women, the story of the disobedience to God has been even a more powerful one. The traditional reading introduces the woman speaking to the devil by herself and then tempting the man to sin. But Trible has proposed a more careful reading for our consideration. The serpent uses plural forms when speaking, indicating that the man and woman were together. The woman, who answers, is described in much greater detail than the man. She "saw that it was good for food, and was a delight to the eyes, and that the tree was to be desired to make one wise" (3:6). We have an image of an intelligent person, attracted by the tree's ability to provide nutrition, by its beauty, and by the possibility of attaining wisdom. She also "builds a fence" around the Torah, saying that not only were they forbidden to eat from the tree, but they should not even touch it. This technique for protecting the law was highly developed later by rabbis. Of the man, we know only that he took and ate.

Regarding the judgment of God, only the serpent and the earth are cursed. Neither the man nor the woman are. Her punishment is pain in childbirth, longing for the original oneness with the man who rules over her. God describes the consequences of their sin. God does not *prescribe* these as a punishment. The oneness (bone of my bone, flesh of my flesh) has been destroyed. Both are corrupted. "His supremacy is neither a divine right nor a male prerogative. Her subordination is neither a divine decree nor the female destiny. Both their positions result from shared disobedience."[17]

In this interpretation, woman was created simultaneously with and equal to man, not for his benefit. Both are responsible for disobedience. Both share in the consequences of that sin. The domination of women by men is recognized, not as the will of God, but as the result of sin. Our responsibility, then, is to overcome the effects of sin and eliminate that relationship of domination/subordination wherever it exists.

### Reclaiming the She-Devil[18]

While not of biblical origin, there is an ancient Jewish folktale associated with the creation myth that suggests that Eve was Adam's second wife. Lilith, the first woman, because of her arrogance and disobedience to Adam, was exiled and came to be known as a demon. She was especially powerful during menstruation, pregnancy, and childbirth. She stole babies from their cribs, was responsible for nocturnal emissions, and castrated men as they slept. Bowls from the sixth century are inscribed with incantations against Lilith. Medieval amulets worn by both Christians and Jews give testimony to the power of her myth. She is mentioned in the Talmud and has been mentioned by such writers as Dante Gabriel Rossetti and Anatole France. In all cases, Lilith is an evil she-devil intent upon sexual destruction.

Judith Plaskow Goldenberg has effected another revision of the myth. It is an allegory for what is happening among women today as the walls that have separated them are overcome. Adam's first wife, Lilith, was equal to Adam in all ways but he ordered her around, expected to be waited on and left the messy jobs for her to do. When Lilith, not liking the situation, flew away leaving Adam to fend for himself, he complained to God about the uppity woman. God caused a deep sleep to fall on him and made Eve from one of his ribs. Things went well for a while, but Eve occasionally sensed capacities within herself that were not developed; she was also disturbed by the exclusive relationship between God and Adam.

Meanwhile, Lilith thought she might like to rejoin the human community, but at every attempt Adam shored up the walls and even did battle with her to keep her out. He told Eve that Lilith was a demon who threatened women in childbirth and stole children from their cradles in the middle of the night. One day, Eve climbed a tree and swung over the garden wall and met Lilith. She recognized a creature like unto herself, not a demon at all. They talked and laughed and cried, and the bonds of sisterhood grew between them. "And God and Adam were expectant and afraid the day Eve and Lilith returned to the garden, bursting with possibilities, ready to rebuild it together."[19]

### Reclaiming the Slave Woman[20]

It is no accident that one of the studies on Hagar is done by Elsa Tamez, a Mexican feminist scholar. Tamez writes from the position of advocacy for the oppressed and disenfranchised. In reading Genesis 16:1–4; 21:8–20, she focuses not on Sarai and Abram, the rich and powerful Israelites, but on Hagar, the foreign slave woman. She was a foreigner, a slave, and a woman, and was thus triply oppressed. In traditional studies, Hagar is a negative model since she was rebellious, would not obey Sarai, and was even accused of looking upon Sarai with contempt. Hagar was Sarai's slave and as such served much as a personal maid might today. She could also be called upon to serve as wet nurse for the children of her mistress. She could even be given to Abram to bear a child for Sarai. Barren, Sarai gave "her to Abram, her husband, as a wife" (Gn 16:3).

As the story unfolds, Hagar became pregnant and looked at

Sarai with contempt. Sarai demanded that she be demoted from concubine to slave once more and began to mistreat her. Unwilling to tolerate such abuse, Hagar ran away to the desert where she was visited by an angel of the Lord who asked about her past and her future. "Hagar, maid of Sarai, where have you come from and where are you going?" When she replied that she was fleeing from her cruel mistress, the angel told her to return to her mistress. It appears that God was on the side of the oppressors. But, perhaps God was insuring that Hagar and her son would be saved. In the desert they might both die, but in the house of Abram they would at least live. "Hagar must wait a little longer, because Ishmael must be born in the house of Abram to prove that he is the first born and to enter into the household through the rite of circumcision. This will guarantee him participation in the history of salvation, and will give him rights of inheritance in the house of Abram."[21] The angel promised Hagar that her descendants will be so numerous that they will not be able to be counted. She is the only woman in the Hebrew scriptures to have such a promise made; customarily that promise is given to the father. She is also the only woman to have a theophany, a vision of God. She asked, "Have I really seen God and remained alive after seeing him?" (16:13). Hagar bestows a name upon God: *El Roi*, the God of seeing.

But life was not easy for Hagar and her son Ishmael. When Sarai had a son, Isaac, she became jealous of Hagar and forced Abram to evict "this slave woman with her son; for the son of a slave woman shall not be heir with my son Isaac" (21:10). Traditional readings of this story overlook the cruelty and harshness of both Abram and Sarai, thereby insinuating that the sins and failings of the powerful are somehow to be tolerated in order to fulfill the will of God. But, reading from the perspective of the oppressed allows no such luxury. Abram sent Hagar and Ishmael into the desert with some bread and a skin of water. When the water had been used up and Hagar could no longer bear to hear the cries of her child, she put him in the shade under a bush and sat a distance from him because she could not stand to see the death of her son. Once more, God sent an angel to comfort her.

This time the question is not about the past or the future but only about the present: "What troubles you, Hagar? Fear not." God gave solace and another promise that her son would be father of a great nation. Hagar was put in the traditional role of the father, taking the boy with a strong hand and raising him to be "a wild ass of a man" (16:12). Tamez takes this to mean "that Ishmael will be one who will not be dominated or domesticated, as his mother before him.... No one will be able to ignore him, and all will know the great injustice that was done to him and his mother in trying to erase them from history."[22]

There are a number of parallels between Abram and Hagar. They both were forced to leave their homes (12:1 and 21:14). They both received a promise from Yahweh that their descendants would be too numerous to count (15:5 and 16:10). Each was faced with the prospect of the death of a son. Abram was willing to carry it out himself, but Hagar could not bear to see her boy die (22:9 and 21:16,18). And finally, they both had theophanies. The Lord appeared to Abram and said, "I am the God Almighty [El Shaddai, the God of the mountain]." When the Lord spoke to Hagar, it was she who named God: "Thou art the God of seeing [El Roi] " (16:13). But through the centuries, Father Abraham, the patriarch, has been revered and honored, and Hagar has been ignored by both Jews and Christians. She is honored by Muslims, however, as the mother of Ishmael. At the time of the hegira to Mecca, a "lesser pilgrimage" is undertaken, walking back and forth from hill to hill, in memory of Hagar searching for water to save her son.

Hagar has been claimed as the patron of homeless people, driven from shelter by the powerful, even the virtuous powerful. She is also a model for many women left with the responsibility of children by uncaring fathers. She complicates the history of salvation and forces us to recognize and condemn the actions of one of Israel's patriarchs.

### Reclaiming the Queens[23]

Vashti is probably the least known of all the outrageous women in scripture. She was the wife of King Ahasuerus who reigned from India to Ethiopia and is the main character in the first chapter of the book of Esther. She has recently been reclaimed, especially by Jewish feminist biblical scholars, as a model for women. Esther's exploits at saving her people are celebrated each year at Purim, a feast during which games, songs, and costumes pass on the story to the next generation of Jewish children. Girls and boys dress up in costumes as they try on the biblical characters: They might be the king, who is portrayed as powerful, proud, and arrogant; or Mordecai, Esther's uncle, who is courageous, learned, and pious; or Esther who is beautiful, humble, loyal, and obedient.

The story recorded in the Book of Esther and celebrated at Purim goes thus: King Ahasuerus gave a great banquet that lasted seven days, and he invited powerful nobility to enjoy his hospitality. Fine linen, couches of gold and silver on mosaic pavements, marble, and precious stones were the backdrop for the lavish feast. Queen Vashti gave her own feast for the women, who were forbidden by custom to join their husbands and consorts. On the seventh day, when the king was "merry with wine," he sent for his wife, Queen Vashti, to come with her royal crown and show her beauty to the gathered princes. Vashti refused to come before the drunken company. Infuriated, Ahasuerus asked advice of the wise men present. Since she was a queen and what she did would be proclaimed to all the women of the realm, it was imperative that she be punished or other wives would imitate her. The sage advice was that the king should expel Vashti, give her place to another, and issue a royal decree in the many languages of the kingdom so that all women high and low would give honor to their husbands and that "every man should be lord in his own house" (1:22). Vashti was penalized because of her independence and self determination. She was also made an example for all other women in the realm. Vashti used her power directly and openly and was punished for it. But Esther used her power in a more conventional manner. Esther saved her people through stereotypic female manipulation and the use of "women's wiles."

Esther is rightly exalted and honored for her role in saving the Jewish people. But she is a virtuous woman as described by a male-centered society. She is almost always spoken of in the pas-

sive voice: She was taken to the palace; she was put in custody of
the eunuch; she was provided with ointments, food, and seven
maids; she was moved to the best place in the harem. She asked
for nothing, except what the eunuch or her uncle, Mordacai, told
her to ask for. In this way, she found favor with the authorities
in the harem and with the king, and she was crowned queen.
When Mordacai told her of Haman's plot to kill all Jews, she
dressed in her most beautiful clothes, prepared not one but two
meals for the king, and revealed the plot, thereby putting herself
in jeopardy, since Ahasuerus did not know she was a Jew.

Traditionally, Mordecai is counted as wise, judicious, and
pious, and a hero of this story, but Frieda Clark Hyman sees him
as demonstrating "little wisdom, no judgment and, at best, misguided piety...an obdurate man who had caused the deadly crisis
(all the Jews being at risk of death)."[24] Mordecai refused to bow
to Haman even though there was no law against it. Haman was
so infuriated that he plotted against all Jews. In the crisis, Esther
grew from a frightened compliant little girl to a responsible
adult woman, albeit a woman according to an androcentric model for women. But it is she who is wise, judicious, courageous,
and pious, willing to reveal herself as a Jew and go to the king in
order to save her people. "Rarely has so poorly equipped a woman grappled so heroically with so dangerous a challenge."[25]

Two women; two uses of power; two different consequences.
The message is clear; independence is punished and passive docility is rewarded.

### Reclaiming the Tricksters[26]

I am not using "trickster" in a casual way, but rather in the
way that anthropologists, folklorists, and historians of religions
use it. A trickster is usually a powerless person who outwits
dominant people by guile or trickery and in so doing changes
the course of events.

Evidence from the social sciences suggests that individuals
resort to the use of trickery under certain social conditions.
In particular, when individuals lack authority, whether it
be political, economic, religious, or domestic authority,

they resort to strategies that allow them to achieve their goals and gain compliance with their wishes.[27]

The women historically known as deceivers assume a different image when defined under the category of trickster.

The story connected to the birth of Moses (Ex 1:15–2:10), introduces a whole cast of trickster women. The midwives Shiphrah and Puah did not kill the Hebrew male children as they had been ordered, but reported instead that because the Hebrew women were so healthy they delivered before a midwife arrived. Moses' mother and sister hid him in the weeds on the bank of the river, and when Pharaoh's daughter found him and his sister, she offered to find someone to nurse him. Of course the job went to his own mother. The tangle of trickery casts an even wider web. By what trickery could Pharaoh's daughter have raised a Hebrew boy in the palace of Pharaoh? The whole history of the Jewish people begins with women: midwives, mother, sister, and daughter of the Pharaoh, all in some way powerless, who were willing to bend the law and resort to deception in the struggle against domination.

Tamar is another Israelite women who resorted to deceit and trickery in order to realize what was her due. According to the Leverite Law, if a man died without a son, his brother was obliged to marry the widow in order to raise up a son for the dead man. When Er (Tamar's husband and Judah's wicked first born) died, Judah ordered Onan to "perform the duty of a brother-in-law to her" (Gn 38:8). But Onan, not wanting to give his brother a child, spilled his seed. He, too, was punished by God and died, leaving his name for all time to the sin of Onanism. Judah, not wanting to risk the life of his third son, sent Tamar home until Shelah would grow up. In due time Tamar realized that Judah was not going to send for her, so she took things into her own hands. She put off her widow's garb, dressed as a prostitute, and waited along the side of the road that she knew Judah would travel. When he promised to send her payment for her services, she demanded a pledge of his signet, his cord, and his staff. Eventually Judah heard that Tamar was pregnant, and he sent for her to be burned since he believed that she had dishonored his house. She produced the signet, cord, and staff, and Judah realized that she was more righteous than he. By her trickery, Tamar received what was her due; in the process she did safeguard the patriarchal structure, but she also challenged the idea that only men contributed to the accomplishment of the promises of God to Israel. Tamar is an ancestor of David and also of Jesus. She is one of four women whom Matthew mentions in his genealogy of Jesus (Mt 1:1–17).

Both men and women in the bible use trickery or deception, but often women's deception is distinguished from men's by three strategies: No motivation is attributed to women, no judgment is made, and there is no confrontation, and therefore no closure. Esther Fuchs makes the point:

> By suppressing motivation, the narrator makes it difficult for the reader to exonerate the female deceiver. By suspending judgment, the narrator creates a kind of ambiguity which may lead to a paleosymbolic association of femininity and deceptiveness. The absence of closure contributes to this vagueness, suggesting that in the case of women, deception is not a problem requiring punishment or reformation.[28]

The narrative recorded in Genesis 31 speaks of two deceptions: Jacob's and Rachel's. Jacob, when he realized that his father-in-law no longer looked on him with favor, waited until Laban had left to shear his sheep, and took all that he had: sons, wives, and cattle, and set out to return to his father Isaac. Laban, upon hearing this, pursued the caravan and accused Jacob of cheating him and of depriving him of bidding his daughters farewell. They eventually make a covenant, bringing the episode to closure.

Not so with Rachel who took one of her father's idols. We don't know if she took it for its monetary value, or if she did not want to leave her household god behind, or if she wanted revenge on her father. Jacob's deception was one of self defense against an unjust Laban; Rachel's unmotivated stealing appears arbitrary. Jacob's action was justified because he has been mistreated and things were getting worse. No justification is given for Rachel's behavior. The covenant between father and son-in-law closes the Jacob story, but in the case of Rachel we are left with her statement: "I have the way of women" (a euphemism for menstruation). She had hidden the idol in a camel's saddle and was sitting on it when her father came to search for it. Because a menstruating woman was *nidda*, ritually unclean, everything she touched was unclean. Her father could not touch her nor the saddle upon which she sat. We don't know if her words were another deception, but they serve to associate menstruation and deception. There is no confrontation, compromise, or punishment for Rachel. Her deception appears "the way of women."

### Reclaiming the Victim[29]

The unnamed woman in chapters 19 and 20 of the book of Judges is memorialized by Phyllis Trible with the inscription: "Her body was broken and given to many." She was a concubine apparently with a mind of her own. Angry at her husband, she returned to her father's house and stayed there until her husband came "to speak kindly to her" (19:3). He stayed five days in her father's house and he and his father-in-law ate and drank and had many conversations. We are never told whether he spoke to the woman, kindly or not. After repeated urgings to remain, the man, his servant, and the woman unwisely set out on their journey at nightfall. When they could go no farther because of the darkness, they were given hospitality by an old man in Gibeah. As they were eating and drinking, Benjaminites beat on the door and demanded that they be allowed to have sex with the visitor. The host, horrified at this request, said that they could have his virgin daughter and the concubine instead. "Ravish them and do with them what seems good to you; but against this man do not do so vile a thing"(19:24). We wonder if the use of the words good and vile in the same sentence is paradoxical.

Then, the husband—he of the kindly words—"seized his concubine, and put her out to them" (19:25). They raped and abused her all night; at dawn they left, and she crawled to the door of the house. Her husband put her on an ass and headed for home.

When he arrived home, he hacked her into twelve pieces and sent them to the tribes of Israel. Trible suggests, contrary to popular reading, that he may be her murderer. She has been pictured as dying on the doorstep, but nowhere does it say that she died there. Violence begets violence. Israel waged war on the Benjaminites, killing thousands upon thousands. Then, needing wives for the Benjaminites who survived the battle, they murdered the men and women of a town that had not participated in the fighting, leaving only four hundred virgins who were turned over to the Benjaminites as wives. Four hundred were not enough, so two hundred more virgins from Shiloh who had come to dance in the yearly festival of Yahweh were kidnapped. The rape of one became the killing of many thousands and the rape of six hundred more. Trible eulogizes:

> Of all the characters in scripture, she is the least. Appearing at the beginning and close of a story that rapes her, she is alone in a world of men. Neither the other characters nor the narrator recognizes her humanity. She is property, object, tool and literary device. Without name, speech or power, she has no friends to aid her in life or mourn her in death. Passing her back and forth among themselves, the men of Israel have obliterated her totally. Captured, betrayed, raped, tortured, murdered, dismembered, and scattered, this woman is the most sinned against.[30]

Trible laments the silence that has been the response to this text both in the rest of the bible and through the ages, even though the story orders, "direct your heart to her, take council and speak" (19:30). In her memory we must speak to the violence inflicted upon women today: captured, betrayed, raped, tortured, murdered, dismembered, and scattered.

The litany of names we have just read: Eve, Lilith, Vashti, Esther, Hagar, Tamar, Rachel, and the unnamed concubine are all characters in texts written in a male-centered period. The narrators and the early readers probably did not understand the women as they have been presented here, but the bible, more than most good literature, may be read on many levels with different meanings and interpretations. In reclaiming and memorializing the women in scripture, feminist scholars are questioning traditional renditions, calling attention to the androcentricity of the bible, and raising up models for women today. As we read or hear the word preached, the "hermeneutics of suspicion" will preclude a naive and uncritical acceptance of traditional images of women.

### Questions for Reflection

1. How would you answer a person who claims that the scriptures are so misogynous as to be unusable by today's women?

2. A "hermeneutic of suspicion" suggests that there are parts of the bible that we must be on our guard against. Do you agree with that position? Can you think of a particular section that this applies to?

3. How has the creation story been used against women? Have you felt the effects of a negative presentation of Eve?

4. Choose one of the women discussed in this chapter and try to imagine the story from her perspective. If possible, share your interpretation with someone else.

5. What is your reaction to the stories of Lilith, Vashti, Esther, Hagar, Tamar, Rachel, and the unnamed concubine? Have you ever focused on these stories in the past? With what results?

### Endnotes

1. Quoted in "Michelangelo's Sistine Ceiling: To Clean or Not to Clean?" by Jane Dillenberger and John Dillenberger in *Bible Review* 4 (August 1988) 14.

2. Ibid., 19.

3. Carolyn Osiek, "The Feminist and the Bible: Hermeneutical Alternatives" in *Feminist Perspectives on Biblical Scholarship* edited by Adela Yarboro Collins (Chico, CA: Scholars Press, 1985) 98.

4. Eugene C. Ulrich and William Thompson, "The Tradition as a Resource in Theological Reflection—Scripture and the Minister" in *Method in Ministry* by James D. Whitehead and Evelyn Eaton Whitehead (New York: Seabury, 1983) 41.

5. Pheme Perkins, "Women in the Bible and Its World" in *Interpretations: A Journal of Bible and Theology*, January 1988, 32.

6. If you are not familiar with the bible, you may want to have one handy in order to read the texts that we will discuss in this chapter.

7. Rosemary Radford Ruether, *Sexism and God-Talk: Toward a Feminist*

Theology (Boston: Beacon Press, 1983) 24.

8. Ibid., 23.

9. Elisabeth Schüssler Fiorenza, "The Will to Choose or to Reject: Continuing Our Critical Work" in Feminist Interpretations of the Bible edited by Letty Russell (Philadelphia: Westminster, 1985) 130.

10. Ibid., 130-131.

11. Katie Geneva Cannon, "The Eminence of Black Feminist Consciousness" in Russell, Feminist Interpretation, 31.

12. See Phyllis Trible, God and the Rhetoric of Sexuality (Philadelphia: Fortress Press, 1978) for an exciting and creative discussion of Genesis 1 to 3.

13. Quoted in Rosemary Radford Ruether, "Misogynism and Virginal Feminism in the Fathers of the Church, in Religion and Sexism edited by Rosemary Radford Ruether (New York: Simon and Schuster, 1974) 157.

14. Trible, God and the Rhetoric of Sexuality, 10.

15. Ibid., 80.

16. Ibid., 94.

17. Ibid., 128.

18. See Roslyn Lacks, Women and Judaism: Myth, History and Struggle (Garden City, N.Y.: Doubleday, 1980) and Judith Plaskow Goldenberg, "Epilogue: 18. The Coming of Lilith" in Religion and Sexism edited by Rosemary Radford Ruether (New York: Simon and Schuster, 1974).

19. Ibid., 343.

20. See Phyllis Trible, Texts of Terror (Philadelphia: Fortress Press, 1984); Elsa Tamez, "The Woman Who Complicated the History of Salvation" in Cross Currents Summer, 1986; Carol Ochs, Women and Spirituality (Totowa, NJ: Rowman and Allanheld, 1983) 34-40.

21. Tamez, "The Woman Who Complicated History," 137.

22. Ibid., 139.

23. See Mary Gendler, "The Restoration of Vashti" in The Jewish Woman edited by Elizabeth Koltun (New York: Schocken Books, 1976) 241-247; Frieda Clark Hyman, "The Education of a Queen" in Judaism 35:1 (Winter 1986).

24. Ibid., 78 and 81.

25. Ibid., 85.

26. See Naomi Steinberg, "Israelite Tricksters, Their Analogues and Cross Cultural Study" in Semeia 42 (1988) 1-13; Johanna W.H. Bos, "Out of the Shadows" in Semeia 42 (1988) 37-67; Esther Fuchs, "'For I Have the Way of Women': Deception, Gender and Ideology in Biblical Narrative" in Semeia, 42 (1988) 68-83; Esther Fuchs, "Who is Hiding the Truth? Deceptive Women and Biblical Androcentrism" in Feminist Perspectives on Biblical Scholarship edited by Adela Collins (Chico, CA: Scholars Press, 1985) 137-144.

27. Steinberg, "Israelite Tricksters," 6.

28. Fuchs, 'For I Have the Way of Women,' 70.

29. See Trible, Texts of Terror.

30. Ibid., 80-81.

# Women in the Apostolic Writings

**I** have already emphasized the fact that the scriptures are documents written by men to be read by men. If we recall the attitude of the male followers of Jesus regarding women, we can more readily understand what to expect in their writings. They were surprised that Jesus would talk to the woman at the well, even though she herself was surprised that a Jew would talk to a Samaritan. They tried to send the Syro-Phoenician woman away. They complained about the mothers who brought the children to Jesus. They protested against the woman who anointed Jesus. Can we expect that they would have made women central to their narratives? The wonder is that there are as many hints as there are. Sandra Schneiders writes that although the scriptures do play a privileged role in our effort to engage divine revelation, it is "the limited, necessarily biased, and sometimes erroneous testimony of believers, who though enjoying a privileged role in the plan of God, were restricted by their personalities, their historical and cultural setting, and their language in both their experience of Jesus and their witness to that experience...."[1]

As scriptural studies about women have advanced, and as the scriptures are put in dialogue with the experience of Christian women today, we are beginning to discover the roles women played, this in spite of the overwhelming androcentric disposition of the translators, preachers, liturgists, and even the authors of the scriptures. Elisabeth Schüssler Fiorenza warns that: "androcentric tendencies of traditional and contemporary interpretations are not completely read into the text; rather, they are generated by it."[2]

An indication of the androcentric mind-set operative in the church today is the adoption of the *Common Lectionary* by Roman Catholic, Episcopal, Presbyterian, Lutheran, and United Methodist churches in Canada and the United States. A study of that lectionary undertaken by Marjorie Proctor-Smith[3] indicates that it fails to take women seriously as active and significant agents in salvation history. The lectionary is a selective document, designed to omit what is irrelevant, inappropriate, or even morally offensive to today's readers. We do not, for example, tell slaves to be subject to their masters, but we do read Ephesians 5:21–33, which commands wives to be subject to their husbands as to the Lord. In the three-year cycle of readings, Peter's confession that Jesus is the Son of God is read in all three years, but the anointing of Jesus by the woman (in all four gospels) is read only once. The primacy of Peter among the disciples may need to be emphasized but it ought not to be stressed to the detriment of other disciples.

That women are seen as peripheral to the passion narrative is obvious since the story of the Messianic anointing of Jesus by the woman is not included in Year A and may be omitted in Year B when the shorter version is read. In all three years of the liturgical cycle, the witness of the women at the burial of Jesus may be omitted when the shorter reading is used. "Evidently the women's role was not regarded by the compilers as essential to the proclamation of the passion and death of Jesus."[4] Sunday readings are not meant to be academic or critical studies. They are surrounded with symbols and words of respect and are for the edification of the Christian community. They are meant to call forth from us a positive response, when it is announced "This is the Word of the Lord." Perhaps we would be more honest at times to respond, "No, it is not."

The work of feminist theologians, both male and female, takes on greater urgency in the light of such conscious or unconscious male-centered use of scripture and theology. In reading and listening to the scriptures, we need to keep in mind the cultures in which they were written; the subsequent cultures in which they were interpreted and passed on to us, as well as the culture of our own day. In this chapter we will discuss some of the research done by feminist biblical scholars, male and female, as they bring into conversation the experience of women today and the biblical tradition available to us.

### Paul: For Better or for Worse

The name of Paul, Apostle to the Gentiles, is usually the first mentioned in a discussion such as this. Great efforts are being made to defend Paul against the charge expressed by George Bernard Shaw that he is "the eternal enemy of women." Writers like Robin Scroggs maintain: "It is time, indeed it is past time, to say loudly and clearly that Paul is, so far from being a chauvinist, the only certain and consistent spokesman for the liberation and equality of women in the New Testament."[5] It is as though we are incapable of thinking of Paul as inconsistent, or even wrong, or that his professed theology of equality in Christ sometimes outstripped his operative theology.

Fundamentalists hold to a literal reading and claim that every word in the bible is to be followed. Paul therefore presents a problem for women. But there are other approaches to the study of Paul that fall generally into three categories: claiming that Paul is not the author of offensive passages; reading the text as culture-bound and therefore not binding on us; and third, seeing Paul as struggling, sometimes unsuccessfully, against chauvinism.[6] I do not see these approaches as mutually exclusive. Where research indicates that Paul is not the original writer, we would be foolish to insist on his authorship. It would be equally foolish to think that Paul and his theology were unaffected by the times in which he lived, which of course means that patriarchal attitudes influenced his thinking. Paul, like the rest of us, may not always have been able to live up to the high ideals of the message of Jesus.

Most scripture scholars agree that Paul did not write all of the letters attributed to him. The letters to Timothy and to Titus, called the pastoral epistles, are recognized as written by a follower of Paul, probably close to the end of the first century. The authorship of the epistle to the Colossians is also disputed. It was ordinary procedure for a disciple to write in the name of the master. The presumption was that the spirit of Paul had been absorbed sufficiently that the message was one which he might have written in the same circumstances. Be that as it may, the epistles have been accepted into the official canon of scripture and have been taught and preached through the centuries.

### No Longer Discipleship of Equals[7]

I have already discussed in chapter three the community around Jesus as a discipleship of equals. We can infer from some passages in the first letter to the Corinthians and the later pastoral letters, that after the death and resurrection of Jesus, the communities had begun to be as influenced by the norms of their society as they were by the gospels. Often, religious motivation was assigned to bolster the *status quo*. This appears so in passages referring to women and their place in the Christian communities.

The tone of these epistles is quite different from the four gospels. Nowhere in the gospels are there different admonitions, commands, or regulations for women than for men. Nowhere do we read that Jesus set up one set of teachings for men and another for women. Nowhere do we read that the physiology of women was significant to Jesus. The same call is given to both; the same challenge to follow Jesus; the same measure of discipleship. Only in the epistles does there appear a dichotomy between what it means to be a female disciple and a male disciple.

Scripture scholars do not question the Pauline authorship of the letters to the Corinthians. The problem is to make sense of the restrictions in passages such as 1 Corinthians 11:2–16 in the light of the baptismal formula of Galatians 3:27–28: "As many of you as were baptized into Christ have clothed yourselves with Christ. There is no longer Jew or Greek, there is no longer slave or free, there is no longer male and female; for all of you are one in Christ Jesus."

Paul's admonition (1 Cor 11:2–16) about women keeping their heads covered has been the topic of controversy through the ages. More so now. Paul wrote that the head of every woman is her husband even as Christ is the head of every man. Praying, therefore, with her head uncovered dishonors her head. Paul gives a long list of reasons for covering her head, including for the sake of the angels and nature itself. His last argument is that the custom is carried out in other churches. *Harper's Bible Commentary* submits that "Paul concludes this mixture of biblical and philosophical arguments with an authoritarian assertion in v. 16, probably because he senses that his theological argument is not very convincing."[8] Be that as it may, this passage has a long history of being used to keep women subject to their husbands because that very subjection is connected to Christ and God.

The author of the first letter to Timothy exhorts men to pray without anger or quarreling. Women, on the other hand, received a list of directives: They should not adorn themselves with fine jewels; be submissive and learn in silence; and not presume to teach or have authority over men. The reason given is that Eve, not Adam, was deceived and transgressed. It is the only time in scripture that the interpretation of the myth of Adam and Eve is used to subordinate women. The chapter ends with the announcement that women will be saved by childbearing. This, in spite of the example of Jesus, who did not identify women by what they did or did not do with their bodies (2:1–14).

The letter to Titus also includes behaviors and virtues that are different for men than for women. Older men are to be temperate, serious, sensible, sound in faith, love, and steadfastness. Older women are also to be reverent in behavior but are encouraged to avoid slander and drink. They are also to teach the young women to love their husbands and to be sensible, chaste, domestic, kind, and submissive to their husbands that the word

of God may not be discredited. The domesticating and taming of
the gospel message had begun. Might it be that when women
took the liberating message of the gospels seriously, they no
longer played the culturally assigned roles of subordination? It
hardly seems that the author would have written about subordination unless some in the community found insubordination
a problem.

### The Unattached Woman

In the first letter to Timothy (chapter 5), we read that "true
widows" who have no family to care for them should be taken
care of by the community. The underside of this command is
that each man is instructed to provide for his own family or be
considered worse that an unbeliever, a far cry from the community described in the Acts of the Apostles where everything
was held in common and no one was in need. There has been
controversy whether this reference to widows indicates that an
order of widows, official ministers, had already been established.
It may well be that they were invested with some clerical functions, but the point here is that widows, too, were judged by
their reproductive functions. No widow under the age of sixty
could be enrolled, for when they "grow wanton against Christ,
they desire to marry" (5:11). Moreover, they become gossipers,
busybodies, and idlers. Again, let them marry and have children.

Adela Yarbro Collins writes from the perspective of a twentieth-century American feminist, but her remarks apply equally to
the women of the first century to whom the epistle was addressed.

> ...the Bible and related traditions seem to offer women a
> difficult choice: either marriage and children without an ac-
> tive public life or an active public life outside the home, but
> as a single celibate.... The dual tradition...raises for us in a
> vivid and graphic way the problem which has been ex-
> pressed in the aphorism, "Biology is destiny." Our role in
> reproduction makes our leadership beyond the family
> problematic, if not impossible.[9]

**Paul and Women Leaders**

The first convert in Europe was a woman. Paul met Lydia, a merchant in Asia, when he arrived in Philippi. An international trader, Lydia was in all likelihood a wealthy woman. Her home was large enough to have Paul, Timothy, Luke, and Silas as guests for an extended stay. She was a "worshipper of God," a Gentile with some connections to the synagogue. She and all her household received baptism at the hands of Paul. It is thought that the church at Philippi probably met in her home, the cradle of Christianity in Europe (Acts 16:13–15). Two other women at Philippi call for Paul's attention (Phil 4:2–3). He feared that the disagreement between Evodia and Syntyche, both of whom struggled at his side in promoting the gospel, might disrupt the community. Even the negative mention of them gives witness to their position in the community.

Paul commends Phoebe to the Romans (16:1), and he calls her sister, *diakonos*, and *prostatis*. *Diakonos*, a term Paul uses for himself and Apollos, is usually translated "missionary," "minister," or "servant." *Prostatis* may mean a person with authority, a protector, a patron with social and political influence. Some translations render her as "helper" or "benefactor," which of course does not imply a person of authority.[10]

Two missionariy couples receive special mention. Prisca and Aquila, tentmakers like Paul, risked their necks for him (Rm 16:3–4) and taught "God's new way to the learned Apollos" (who only knew the baptism of John). Andronicus and Junia, "prominent among the apostles" were in prison with him. They were not converts of Paul but were in Christ before him (Rm 16:3–4, 7).

The early Christian community included women as well as men as missionaries, preachers, teachers, and leaders. They are called sister, apostle, minister, patron, and co-worker. While there are only a few references to women in the New Testament, the same may be said about men leaders. "One could say that the more independent a woman [or a man] missionary was from the Pauline mission, the less chance she had to be remembered in history, since only the Pauline letters break the silence about the earliest beginnings of the Christian missionary movement."[11]

### Women Disciples of Jesus

When you read the word "disciple" do you conjure up women as well as men in the company of Jesus? In the same sentence, Luke tells us that the twelve and some women were with Jesus. He says specifically that women followed him from town to town, ministered to him, and supported him (Lk 8:2–3). We have the names of some of his disciples: Martha and her sister Mary, Mary from Magdala, Joanna who was the wife of Herod's steward, and Susanna. According to Luke, there were "many others who provided for them out of their means." Jesus himself speaks of his disciples as his family: "Whoever does the will of God is my mother and brother and sister" (Mk 3:35). He included Mary, the sister of Martha, among those whom he taught, and this was at a time when, most, but not all, rabbis would have denied women the right to study the Torah.

Elisabeth Schüssler Fiorenza describes the community around Jesus as the discipleship of equals where the patriarchal model of power over others is abolished. Given that setting and conscious of family orientation of Jewish ritual feasts, it is unlikely that at the last meal that Jesus shared with his disciples, only men would have been present, no matter what DaVinci thought.

It may even be possible that the disciples on the road to Emmaus after the crucifixion (Lk 24:13–35), were husband and wife. There is ample evidence that families went up to Jerusalem to celebrate the Holy Days together, and we can conjecture that when they invited Jesus to "Stay with us for it is toward evening and the day is far spent," they had arrived at their own house. It is unlikely that two Jewish men would have lived together. The more likely scenario is that wife and husband experienced the death and resurrection appearance of Jesus together. We are as free to speculate that the disciples were a married couple as are others to conjecture that it was two men. We have to erase centuries of religious art, the product of a patriarchal society, from our imaginations and replace it with a more inclusive image.

### Mary, the Woman from Magdala[12]

Was ever a woman more maligned and slandered than Mary? She is the only woman mentioned by name in all four gospels.

What we know specifically of Mary from Magdala is that she followed Jesus from town to town (Lk 8:2; Mt 27:56; Mk 15:41); she remained at the foot of the cross and was present when Jesus was buried (Mt 27:56, 61; Mk 15:40,47; Jn 19:25), and that she was first witness to the resurrection (Mt 28:1; Mk 16:1,9; Lk 24:10; Jn 20:1,18). Mary is mentioned in five of the six resurrection gospel narratives, and when she is mentioned she is always the first named. The only gospel resurrection story in which she is not present is the appearance of Jesus to the disciples who have been fishing on the Sea of Tiberias (recorded in the appendix of John's gospel). Paul emphasizes the authority of Peter and the apostles when he ignores Magdalen in his list of those who have had an experience of the risen Christ. He writes, "he appeared to Cephas, then to the twelve. Then to the more than five hundred brethren at one time...." (1 Cor 15:5–6).

The fact that all four evangelists record her relationship with Jesus gives witness to the significance of Jesus in her life and of her in Jesus' life. When we discussed her in one of my classes and intuited her devotion and fidelity to Jesus, one of my students said, "Imagine what effect the love of such a woman had on Jesus!" Imagine, indeed.

And yet her name has become synonymous with prostitute and harlot. In spite of her fidelity, she is remembered as a sinner. Of course, for a woman to be a sinner implies some kind of suspect sexual activity. We do not think of her as unjust or unfaithful or unkind. A woman's sin is always sexual. Her reputation as a sinner flows from the statement that she was the woman "from whom he had cast out seven demons" (Lk 8:2; Mk 16:9). This has been interpreted to mean that Jesus had cast out sin, and grievous sin at that, from her. But the *New Jerome Biblical Commentary* explains simply that it means a "restoration to health."[13] In other cases where casting out demons is recorded, it is understood to mean some kind of cure. Only in the case of Mary are we left with the reputation of a loose (but converted) woman. The image of a faithful woman who suffered at the crucifixion and to whom Jesus chose to appear before all others seems to be more than a patriarchal society could comprehend.

Using a "hermeneutics of creative actualization," Renata

Weems understands Mary Magdalen differently. The gospels present her as a significant figure and the apocryphal Gospel of Mary describes a charismatic leader. She was a woman too gifted for the constraints of her society, who became sick because she could not express herself, could not be herself. "Imagine: Here was an otherwise gifted, intelligent, bright, charismatic woman living in a society which had no place for gifted, intelligent, bright, charismatic women."[14] Unable to use her gifts, she fell ill. The seven demons who possessed her were "depression, fear, low self-esteem, doubts, procrastination, bitterness, and self-pity."[15] But something Jesus said or did broke through and freed her gifts to be shared for the good of the community.

We have to ask ourselves why Mary was so defamed. The apocryphal gospels, those not accepted in the official canon, speak of Mary's missionary journeys and hint at jealousy and conflict between the followers of Peter and her followers, a case similar to the friction between the disciples of John the Baptist and Jesus' disciples. It has been suggested that her reputation was slandered in order to advance the dominant position of Peter and to minimize hers. It may also be that in a church that was espousing celibacy as a way of life for many, presenting her as a sinner provided some distance between her and Jesus.

There are some who believe that we may have been focusing on the wrong Mary, that the focus on the mother dimension may be too one-dimensional. Mary Magdalen, as friend and disciple of Jesus, was honored in some early Christian communities as the disciple Jesus loved more than the others. The apocryphal gospel of Mary presents her as a leader and missionary who labored even as did Peter, Paul, and the others whose names have been preserved in official writings. Moltmann-Wendel calls attention to the rich visual material in which the contributions of Mary Magdalen are preserved. "She is the beautiful preacher who is to be seen on medieval pulpits; in a stained-glass window in Chalone-sur-Marns she even baptizes; and on an altar triptych in Lübeck, she makes her brother a bishop."[16] Restoring her reputation as friend, disciple, and missionary could provide hope for the development of new human relationships of the sort we read about in the New Testament.

### The Woman at the Well

Since I have been able to see her through new eyes, the un-named Samaritan woman at the well has become one of my favorite scriptural characters. The setting is in arid country at midday, when the sun is brightest. Since John uses the symbol of light, telling us that Jesus is the light of the world (1:4–5 and 8:12), might it be that the meeting between the woman and Jesus is set at noon to emphasize her entry into the light?

Jesus opens the conversation with a request for water. The woman recognizes him as a Jew and ponders the division between the Jews and her people, the enmity between them. She may have been wondering about Jesus drinking from a cup that Jews would ordinarily call unclean. Jesus moves the conversation from well water to living water. In the light of her intelligence and theological awareness, evident in the subsequent discussion, it is likely that she understood his meaning. She asks for the living water, a common enough symbol for God's Revelation, Wisdom, and Divine Life; even the Torah was described as living water. The living water here is Jesus' teaching and revelation. This woman knows her theology; the conversation, from beginning to end, has to do with religious issues, even the discussion of the five "baals" (usually translated as "husbands" and which lead to the perception of her as a sinner).

I suggest that we look at one of the other possible translations. "Baal" has many meanings: Lord, Master, Husband, God. Let us suppose that Jesus tells her to ask her own god for living water. She replies that she has no god and Jesus agrees, for the Samaritans had strayed from the worship of the one true God in continuing to worship the five pagan gods brought back from captivity with them.[17]

The second book of Kings records the history of the Samaritans' obstinacy regarding their pagan gods.

> But every nation still made gods of its own and put them in the shrines of the high places that the people of Samaria had made, every nation in the cities in which they lived.... So they worshipped the Lord but also served their own gods, after the manner from among whom they had been

carried away. To this day they continue to practice their former customs…. So the nations worshipped the Lord, but they also served their carved images; to this day their children and their children's children continue to do as their ancestors did (17:29–41).

While this description is from a period long before the time of Jesus, it does provide insight into the history of the Samaritans and the reason for hostility between them and the Jewish people.

This translation of "baal" as god makes sense in the light of the tenor of the whole conversation, and also in light of Jesus' general lack of attention to "sexual sins." It is at this point in their theological reflection that a new insight is opened to her. She recognizes Jesus as a prophet, whose only role was to call sinners back to worship of the one true God. Her understanding of him has moved from Jew to Prophet.

I have recently heard another possible interpretation of the five husbands.[18] We know that according to Jewish law, husbands could divorce a wife; wives were not able to divorce husbands. The five husbands might suggest a woman who had been abandoned by men. In either case, there is no reason for assigning responsibility to her or suggesting that she is a sinner. Her husbands, or some of them, may have died; again there is no suggestion that she is responsible for that.

The woman introduces the question of where to pray and receives that beautiful reply that "the hour is coming and now is, when the true worshippers will worship the Father in spirit and in truth"(Jn 4:23). When she speaks of the Messiah, she receives an even greater revelation: "I who speak to you am he." Jew, Prophet, Messiah: Slowly Jesus is revealed to her. As a result of the conversation, she is called to ministry. She leaves her water jar, even as Peter and the others left their boats, their nets, and their father's house. She returns to her town and "many Samaritans from the town believed in him because of the woman's testimony" (Jn 4:39). On the strength of her word, her neighbors recognize Jesus as the Savior of the World. It seems unlikely that the town harlot would have had that kind of influence.

Her understanding of Jesus in the process deepens from Jew, to Prophet, to Messiah, to Savior of the World. The woman returns to her town a changed women, on fire with the good news, with a message for her people that would change them, too, forever.

### The Syro-Phoenician Woman[19] (Mk 7:24–30; Mt 15:20–28)

There is another story that illustrates the influence that a woman had over Jesus. Not just a woman, but a Gentile woman and an uppity one at that. She interrupts Jesus when he had gone into a house and didn't want anyone to know he was there; perhaps he is tired and needs a rest. The urgency of her daughter's illness impels her to interrupt him; she irks the disciples who want to get rid of her. The Syro-Phoenician women is not deterred; her daughter is sick and she is willing to do whatever it takes in order to effect a cure. She even accepts being insulted with equanimity. We can surmise from this that she loves her daughter very much, even though daughters are not as valued in her society as sons.

Both Mark and Matthew record the hard words of the conversation. Jesus, in what sounds like a cold rebuff, announces that he was sent only to the house of Israel; she, a Gentile, is not his concern. He then uses more insulting language in telling her that the Jews (the children), must be fed first. It is not right to take the bread of the children and throw it to the Gentiles (dogs). Even if, as some suggest, the words mean puppies or pets, they are cruel. The woman's quick and quick-witted reply that even the dogs get to eat the crumbs, stops Jesus in his tracks. Her faith has overcome even the affront of the healer. She gives us a powerful example of the benefit of really listening to others even when their saying is hard. Jesus certainly sounds firm in his belief about the primacy of Israel, but because she can hear his words as the understanding of a faithful Jew, she is able to challenge those words in such a way that he could hear her. And because he hears her interpretation, he can understand that his mission extends beyond Israel. She knows he is speaking from the perspective of his Jewish culture and tradition, but her insights help him to expand the understanding of his mission.

Sharon Ringe reminds us: "Her wit, her sharp retort, was indeed her gift to Jesus, a gift that enabled his gift of healing in turn, her ministry that opened up the possibility of his...there appears to be a theological point: It sets forth who Jesus is as the Christ of God."[20] Jesus learns from a poor outcast a new vision of his mission; he is moved to conversion and to action.

Fiorenza argues that:

> This saying ascribed to Jesus, then, argues that the gospel of the basileia...should not be given to gentiles for fear they might misuse it.... The argument...is countered by the woman by referring to the messianic abundance of Christian table community. The gracious goodness of the God of Jesus is abundant enough to satisfy Jews but also the gentiles.[21]

### Martha (Jn 11:1–12:2)

Martha, the nag, the shrew who complains that she is left with the kitchen work while Mary just sits around enjoying Jesus' company, has been the stereotype of the overworked and under-appreciated housewife, too busy to think about the really important things of life. But there is another image so strong that it is a wonder we have been blind to it for so long. John tells us: "Now Jesus loved Martha and her sister and Lazarus" (11:5). Martha is in the primary relationship; Mary is not even mentioned by name. Martha, beloved of Jesus, is a central character in the story of the raising of Lazarus. It is she who keeps the movement flowing. Martha sent for Jesus, went out to meet him while "Mary sat in the house," and announced that Jesus' presence would have been enough to keep Lazarus alive.

The story of the raising of Lazarus may have functioned in the Johannine community to address the problem of the death of believers who had been assured by Jesus of eternal life. Martha represents the community, and in this story she is the person who brings the community through the crisis. It is she who makes Jesus present, and it is she who proclaims Jesus "the Christ, the Son of God, he who is coming into the world" (11:27). The titles by which she identifies Jesus take into consideration the different audiences who would read the gospel. Jews would understand "Christ," the Gentiles would understand "Son of God," and the Samaritans would understand "he who is to come."[22] In the gospel of John, Martha plays the role reserved to Peter in the synoptic gospels. In Matthew 16:15–19, Peter professed belief in Jesus as the Christ, the Son of the living God, and was rewarded with the promise that he was the rock upon which the church would be built. Martha's profession has been lost in the shadow of his.

Martha does not profess her faith because of the raising of Lazarus but because of the words of Jesus revealing himself as the Resurrection and the Life. The use of Martha as representative of the Johannine community does not make sense unless women did function as leaders. "But whatever role women held in the Johannine community, the gospel text as it stands presents Jesus addressing the foundational question to a woman and the woman as making, on her own responsibility, the Christian confession."[23]

We might look at one last mention of Martha at the beginning of Chapter 12. "Six days before the Passover, Jesus came to Bethany where Lazarus was, whom Jesus had raised from the dead. There they made him a supper; Martha served...." Raymond Brown[24] has suggested that since the gospel was written in the 90s when the office of *diakonos* existed in the Johannine community, they would have understood that Martha functioned at table in the manner of those upon whom hands had been laid. Six days before the Passover is a Sunday, the Christian sabbath, another hint that the evangelist was not giving us the name of the waitress.

### The Woman Who Anointed Jesus
(Mt 26:6–13; Mk 14:3–9; Lk 7:36-50; Jn 12:1–11)

Popular tradition has collapsed into one the four versions of the story of the woman who anointed Jesus with precious balm. Matthew and Mark set the dinner in the house of Simon the leper; Luke, written later, sets it in the house of a Pharisee, while John, who is writing even later, places the event in the home of Martha and Mary in Bethany. Matthew and Mark describe the woman anointing the head of Jesus; Luke and John, his feet. In

Mark, "some" complained about the waste of precious ointment; in Matthew, the disciples themselves complain; John has Judas as the griper. Luke, the only one to call her a sinner, does not indicate any complaint about the waste of money but rather that Jesus should have known what sort of woman touched him. In John's gospel, Mary, the sister of Martha, anoints Jesus. The point being made here is that the same story is crafted by each of the evangelists to teach something different.

Each of us has family myths and stories that we use in various ways as the occasion demands. We might tell the story of a parent being punished as a child and we may focus on the wisdom of Grandma who knew what had happened just looking at us, or the focus may be the price of disobedience, or the luxury of forgiveness, or even the humor of the situation from an adult perspective. It is the same story with different messages.

The similarity of the texts in Mark and Matthew indicate that they both used the same sources and/or one another. The unnamed woman anoints the head of Jesus in much the same way that the prophets anointed the kings of Israel. As a reward, Jesus says that wherever the gospel is preached, what she has done will be told in memory of her. It is interesting in light of that promise that we don't even know her name and that she is primarily remembered as a sinner. The words "in memory of her" echo the eucharistic formula "Do this in memory of me" (1 Cor 11:24–25). Elisabeth Schüssler Fiorenza maintains that the remarks regarding "the poor being always with us" would have been understood by a community who knew that Jesus was no longer with them. The words of Mark, "For you always have the poor with you and whenever you will you can do good to them," would have been heard as a challenge that now is the time to do good. The words are also a reminder that God's future, the *basiliea* belongs to the poor.[25]

The lessons from John's version are different. Mary anointed the feet of Jesus with precious ointment and dried them with her hair. Sandra Schneiders evokes three points regarding John's account.[26] First, by connecting Mary's wiping of the feet of Jesus with Jesus' washing the disciples' feet described in the next chapter of John, we recognize Mary as disciple in the strict sense of the word. She whom Luke described as sitting and learning at the feet of Jesus, offers an act of veneration to the master; moreover, she performs an act that Jesus commands the disciples to do for one another. "It seems likely enough that John is deliberately presenting this woman as a disciple of Jesus the Teacher, a role generally forbidden to Jewish women.... It is unlikely that he would have done so unless women in his community were active members...who devoted themselves to sacred study and discussion."[27]

The second point is that John makes note of a male objection to her unusual relationship with Jesus. Mary expressed her devotion in an unconventional way, without asking anyone's permission. She assumed the right to decide what form her ministry would take. Each of the four versions of this story agrees on one point: In each a male or males objected to the woman's action, "which makes one aware of how early the attempt of men to control the discipleship and ministry of women began in the Christian community. Jesus' opinion of male attempts to control the relationship between his women disciples and himself is so clear in the New Testament that one can only wonder at the institutional church's failure to comprehend it."[28]

The third point is that the author of John makes a proleptic (or foreshadowing presentation) of the paschal mystery. Jesus is at supper with beloved disciples and which is served by Martha; a beloved disciple, Lazarus, reclines with Jesus; Judas is present and it is noted parenthetically that he is the one who betrayed Jesus; Mary performs the footwashing which Jesus himself does later. The elements of the coming passion and death are foreshadowed, and women are central to the event.

The scriptures, like classics, contain hidden treasures that the original author may not have intended. Reading someone else's words, really reading them, is to enter into dialogue with them; it is to bring our imagination into play. I am not talking about creating fantasy but rather freeing our imagination so that we are freer to recreate events that we never experienced. A disciplined imagination may sound like an oxymoron but that is exactly what is necessary. Scripture requires that we approach it as a friend. But it also requires Fiorenza's hermeneutics of suspicion. We ask "Is there something here I missed before? Is there some hint I overlooked? Am I frozen in one interpretation that I can't see another?" Asking these questions of myself has enabled me to find hints and clues and evidence about women's centrality to the Christian enterprise. Sometimes the "clues" are so obvious that I find myself thinking, "It could not have been there the whole time. They must have put it in when I wasn't looking!"

### Questions for Reflection

1. Recall a stained-glass window or a painting of Jesus with his disciples. Where are the women? What difference would it make if there were women in the picture?

2. What might your community look like if it took seriously the call to be a "discipleship of equals?" What can you do to facilitate that discipleship?

3. Which women in the company of Jesus are role models for you? Why?

4. Choose a scripture story in which a woman is central and write it from her perspective. In what ways is it now different?

5. What is your attitude toward the "feminine" virtues of nurturing, compassion, and sensitivity? How might we balance them with more assertive ones?

6. Reflect about this problem raised by Adela Collins: "Our role in reproduction makes our leadership beyond the family problematic, if not impossible." What is your reaction to it?

### Endnotes

1. Sandra M. Schneiders, *Beyond Patching: Faith and Feminism in the Catholic Church* (New York: Paulist Press, 1991) 65.
2. Elisabeth Schüssler Fiorenza, *But She Said: Feminist Practices of Biblical Interpretation* (Boston: Beacon Press, 1992).
3. Marjorie Proctor-Smith, "Images of Women in the Lectionary" in *Women: Invisible in the Church and Theology* edited by Elisabeth Schüssler Fiorenza and Mary Collins (Edinburgh: T. & T. Clark, 1985).
4. Ibid., 59.
5. Robin Scroggs, "Paul and the Eschatological Woman," *Journal of the American Academy of Religion* 40 (September 1972) 287.
6. See H. Wayne House, "Neither Male or Female...In Christ Jesus" *Bibliotheca Sacra* 145:577 (Jan.-Mar. 1988) 50.
7. See Fiorenza, *In Memory of Her* and Brendan Byrne, S.J., *Paul and the*

*Christian Woman* (Collegeville, MN: Liturgical Press, 1989). While I appreciate the author's insight into the Pauline corpus, I think that he too easily excuses the restraining of women for the good of the community (p. 91, for example). It has too long been women's lot to be sacrificed for the good of others.

8. Mays, James L. et al, *Harper's Bible Commentary* (San Francisco: Harper & Row, 1988) 1183.

9. Adela Yarbro Collins, "The Gospel and Women," The 1987 Fred O. Francis Memorial Lectures in Religion, Department of Religion, Chapman College, Orange, CA (September 29, 1987).

10. See Fiorenza, *In Memory*, 47-48; 169-171.

11. Ibid., 184.

12. See Elisabeth Moltmann-Wendell, "Motherhood or Friendship?" in *Concilium*; Gerald O'Collins, S.J., and Daniel Kendall, S.J., "Mary Magdalen as Major Witness to Jesus' Resurrection" in *Theological Studies* 48 (1987).

13. Robert J. Karris, O.F.M., "The Gospel According to Luke" in *The New Jerome Biblical Commentary* edited by Raymond Brown, S.S., Joseph A. Fitzmyer, S.J., and Roland A. Murphy, O Carm. Englewood Cliffs, NJ: Prentice Hall, 1990) 697.

14. Renata Weems, *Just a Sister Away: A Womanist Vision of Women's Relationships in the Bible* (San Diego: LuraMedia, 1988) 89.

15. Ibid., 90.

16. Moltmann-Wendel, "Motherhood or Friendship?" 20.

17. See Raymond Brown, *The Anchor Bible: The Gospel According to John* (Garden City, NY: Doubleday, 1966) 171. Brown maintains that John may not have intended this interpretation but given the date of publication, the explanation is all the more significant.

18. This gospel was originally written in Greek, not a language that Jesus knew. The word "baal" was, in all likelihood, the word that would have been used by Jesus in a conversation like this.

19. See Sharon H. Ringe, "A Gentile Woman's Story" in *Feminist Interpretation of the Bible* edited by Letty M. Russell (Philadelphia: Westminster, 1985) and Elisabeth Schüssler Fiorenza, *In Memory of Her* (New York: Crossroad, 1983) 136-137.

20. Ringe, "A Gentile Woman's Story," 71-72.

21. Elisabeth Schüssler Fiorenza, *In Memory of Her: A Feminist Theological Reconstruction of Christian Origins* (New York: Crossroad, 1983) 137-138.

22. Russell, *Feminist Interpretations*, 104.

23. Sandra Schneiders, "Women in the Fourth Gospel and the Role of Women in the Contemporary Church" in *Biblical Theology Bulletin* XII (April 1982) 41.

24. Raymond Brown, "Roles of Women in the Fourth Gospel" in *Theological Studies* 36:4 (December 1975) 690-691.

25. Fiorenza, *In Memory of Her*, 153.

26. Schneiders, "Women in the Fourth Gospel," 42-43.

27. Ibid., 42.

28. Ibid., 42.

# 9

# $\mathcal{F}$eminist $\mathcal{S}$pirituality

An old cartoon shows two Buddhist monks sitting cross-legged in meditation. One looks a bit quizzical and the other is saying, "Nothing happens next. This is it." Humorous at first, we soon realize that there is great wisdom in those words. This is it. Spirituality: Buddhist, Jewish, or Christian, is not about waiting for something to happen. Spirituality is an awareness of "the more than meets the eye" in our daily lives, in the here and now. It refers to the whole of our lives, our deepest convictions, our hopes and dreams, our patterns of thought, our emotions, feelings, and behaviors. Spirituality is a way of living that arises from an appreciation of human life. Spirituality has more to do with being embodied spirits than with being enspirited bodies. I will speak more to that point later. While the word has been used in church circles for centuries, even women and men who do not define themselves as religious speak of their spirituality.

The difficulty in speaking about spirituality is that our language sets spirit and body against each other, separates them. Spirituality as the word is understood today has more to do with the unity and integrity of each human being than the split between spirit and matter. Spirituality has to do with the values that people hold; it has to do with what is ultimate in people's lives, it has to do with what meaning they assign to life. It has to do with how we relate—to ourselves, to other people, to all of creation. For those of us who profess belief in God, it has to do with how we relate to that source of our being.

In this chapter I will speak particularly about Christian spirituality and that branch of Christian spirituality that is called feminist. I will not be addressing the many and varied ways that others relate to what is ultimate in their lives. Some of what I say here may resonate with Jews or Muslims or atheists, but I am speaking out of a specifically Christian perspective, and not just Christian, but feminist Christian. I will speak about what appears to be happening in the lives of many Christian women as they are converted to feminism and attempt to articulate their spirituality in the light of their own experience and interpretation, not in the light of the definitions and interpretations imposed upon them by their culture, including more traditional religious interpretations.

Feminist spirituality is a way of being in the world, a way of expressing convictions, values, hopes, and dreams that takes the lives of women seriously. It is a validation and a celebration of women. That validation and celebration takes many forms and might better be referred to in the plural as feminist spiritualities. Whatever their differences, it seems to me that in their many manifestations, feminist spiritualities share four defining characteristics: they are Incarnate, they are Relational, they are Prophetic, and they are Empowering.

### It Is Incarnate

"Carne" means flesh, body. Feminist spirituality takes the body, the flesh very seriously. There is no unnatural split between body and spirit; no separation of the person into soul and body; no division of life into sacred and secular. It is almost impossible to speak of spirituality or sexuality separately. They are so closely intertwined as to be inseparable. Only the paucity of our language forces us to speak as though they are distinct. Sexuality is not to be equated with the whole of our personhood, but it is a basic and wondrous dimension of that personhood. Sexuality is an inclusive term that encompasses sex but goes beyond it. It is tied to the symbol system by which we make sense of our world. Cultural expectations and psychological development both contribute to one's sexuality.

Through feminism, in the search for themselves as persons, women have come to a realization of the beauty and wonder of their bodies. They have had to forget much of what has been said about the female body through the ages. They have had to erase the negative portraits, drawn by men, some of whom regarded a woman's body as only an instrument for male pleasure and others who saw the female body as a source of sin, a temptation, which are flip sides of the same mentality that regards women as sex objects, as things. We have to reflect carefully on the expression "sex object." This may enable us to understand why so many boys and men disdain and abuse the female body. It is an object. The sense of personhood is missing. Objects may be moved, used, discarded at will with no thought of the effect on the object. An object whose function is sex has nothing to do with relationship, intimacy, or with community.

Lacking a sense of the deep personal and communal meaning of sexuality, using sex as a weapon is easy. Witness the rape of women by soldiers in wars. The few peasant survivors of the American slaughter in My Lai told of watching young soldiers who had been trained for war and hatred, raping girl-children and then viciously cutting their bodies to shreds.[1] The divorce between sex and relationality cannot be described in term of animal behavior. Animals mate to satisfy their urges and for propagation. There is no record of animals mating to punish or to violate. That is only possible when the motivation is undergirded by a worldview that holds women as lesser and as created for the benefit of men.

The church has been guilty of defining women by what they do or do not do with their bodies and has provided a religious rationale for treating women differently. The attitude that regards women as unworthy to enter the "holy sanctuary" reinforces the attitude that women are less than men, are mere objects.

Sexuality, as sense of being incarnate, involves more than genitalia; it involves our whole being as male or female. It determines how we experience the world, how we relate to it and to other persons. Sexuality involves our self image, our self esteem, our very self. How we understand ourselves as bodily creatures colors our appreciation of ourselves as persons. Very few women are as content with their bodies as Miss Piggy, who when she was asked to rate herself on a scale from one to ten replied, "Moi, I'm an eleven." Few women have that sense of themselves (or that sense of humor). Society has drawn a clear picture of what the perfect female body looks like, and less than one tenth of one percent of women fit the image.

The current focus on diets, exercise, and health foods has been so exaggerated that one of the most serious problems among college-age women is the abuse of their own bodies. The language of morality is being adopted to describe eating habits rather than moral behavior. When some women speak of being good, they mean that they did not break their diet. When they are bad, they have eaten the "wrong foods" or the wrong amounts. Anorexia and bulimia are destroying beautiful young bodies, beautiful young women.

Feminist spirituality awakens the senses and sharpens feelings. No longer trapped into denying the body, women are seeing, hearing, tasting, smelling, and touching, and they are reveling in their new found awareness. Feminist rituals and celebrations involve not only the mind but the senses as well. Candles, incense, water, oil, song, dance, and storytelling ritualize women's experiences in totally new ways. It may be that this heightened awareness is the result of focusing on women's lives. They take on new meaning, new significance when claimed by women. Feminist spirituality celebrates bodiliness as normal and natural, part of what God saw as good. Tall and short, fat and skinny, old and young, strong and weak, women's bodies are blessed and reverenced.

Women have been identified with nature and with sexuality, and, for the most part, the identification has been negative. Sex has been described in somewhat sordid terms; we speak of "dirty jokes" when we really mean jokes about sexuality. Anomalously, we say, "Sex is dirty; save it for the one you love." Feminists reject negative connotations about the female body and all its aspects: menses, pregnancy, giving birth, lactation, menopause. They celebrate the sacredness of women's life cycles.

Ordinarily, women's bodily functions are not alluded to in religious rituals. Two, however, come to mind. One is the old Catholic custom of "churching" women after childbirth. It was a blessing of the mother but also a form of cleansing, of readmission to the community. The other is the custom of Jewish women cleansing in the *mikvah* or bath after their period. The language of cleansing and purifying that accompanies each of these ceremonies has nothing to do with physical cleanliness but suggests that childbirth and menses may once have been seen as touching the divine and were held in awe. Yet the *Encyclopedia Judaica* judges that the state of ritual impurity "is considered hateful to God, and man is to take care in order not to find himself thus excluded from his divine presence."[2] What began in awe and reverence for the connection between women's bodies and divinity developed into a devaluation of women, their bodies, and their life-giving potentialities.

Incarnational thinking affirms the goodness of matter—not a naive exaltation of matter that ignores the destructive forces of sin and evil in human beings and human societies, but an acceptance of the creator's view that creation is good, indeed very good. It opposes the belief that the whole world is divided into good and bad, into the spiritual and the bodily. This fallacy is our inheritance from our Greek ancestors; it does not come to us through our Jewish forebears. Judaism has had and still has a more positive view of creation and of human life, including human sexuality. The message that is firmly lodged in all strands of Judaism is that creation is not evil, creation is not repudiated by God, and creation is not devoid of God's presence. "On the contrary, God is seeking us within creation."[3]

The church has never officially endorsed the rejection of creation, of matter, of bodiliness; in fact it condemned Gnosticism and Manicheism which taught that matter is evil; it rejected Docetism which taught that Jesus only appeared to be human because it was unthinkable that God could dwell in evil human flesh. But a great fallacy has entered into the popular religious life of Christians. Because of this great fallacy, we set up a two-tier Christianity in which spirit and matter are set at odds with one another.

In Catholicism the fallacy appeared as a system in which some were called to sanctity in the priesthood or religious life and others were not. The truly holy were the celibate: priests, monks, sisters, and brothers. They were the official pray-ers. When I was a child I was often sent to the nearby Carmelite monastery with a small offering so that the sisters would pray for my mother's intention. She did not think her prayers would be heard by God as readily as those of the good sisters. My mother's understanding of sanctity, like most women and men of her day, had less to do with the way she lived out her life and more to do with those persons, places, and things that were set apart from the daily concerns of "ordinary Christians" and there-fore considered sacred.

The Christian mistake was to separate spirituality and the body, especially sexuality, in such a way that they almost be-came opposing forces. The great fallacy taught that to be truly spiritual, one must deny the body, do penance, suffer, forsake the world. The measure of our love for God was how much we were willing to accept suffering, not only accept but search for it, embrace it. Many feminists and other liberation theologians are now questioning the validity of the exaltation of suffering.

African Americans like Bell Hooks and James Cone ask if God is a white racist. Is God responsible for the maldistribution of wealth, for the violence of the ghetto, for premature death that is the lot of so many in the black community? Latin theologians like Jon Sobrino critique the mystique of the cross that ignores the connection between the life and teaching of Jesus and his death.

Joanne Carlson Brown and Rebecca Parker argue: "To sanc-tion the suffering and death of Jesus, even when calling it unjust, so that God can be active in the world only serves to perpetuate the acceptance of the very suffering against which one is strug-gling.... To argue that salvation can only come through the cross is to make God a divine sadist and a divine child abuser."[4] Jews, too, in light of the Holocaust ask themselves what kind of God would decree such anguish and agony on a people, on God's

own people. Elie Wiesel[5] goes so far as to put God on trial for in-
fidelity to the covenant in not saving the Jews. Wiesel finds God
guilty. As a boy in the concentration camp, he watched as rabbis
conducted such a trial, and came to the same conclusion. When
they were finished, and as they rose to leave, they reminded one
another that it was time for prayer.

All of this is not to deny that suffering may have redemptive
aspects; it is rather to understand that suffering may be clean or
dirty. Clean suffering—the suffering that leads to new life, that is
freely chosen for the good of the community or for the good of
oneself, suffering that is endured in the struggle against injustice—these are clean sufferings. The suffering that accompanies poverty and oppression, the suffering imposed upon
the powerless, the suffering inflicted upon non-human creation
by our greed and selfishness, these are dirty sufferings. It would
be a mistake to think that any suffering appeases God, or pleases
God. God grieves with us in the face of suffering. "God's grief is
as ultimate as God's love. Every tragedy eternally remains and is
eternally mourned....Eternally God sings kaddish for the
world."[6]

Asceticism does have strong roots in the Christian tradition
from the time of the desert mothers and fathers and cannot be
entirely repudiated; but asceticism is better understood as a facet
of our relationship with God and with others rather than a value
in itself. The asceticism required of a Christian has nothing to do
with masochism. Suffering that is redemptive is the suffering
that is borne for the good of others, the suffering that accompanies the struggle for peace, justice, and the coming reign
of God.

A Spartan ascetic view of spirituality is based, in part, on attending more to the Fall than to Creation. It has little to do with
the view of reality as depicted in Genesis. God saw that creation
was good; and after forming human beings, male and female,
God saw that creation was *very* good. A harsh ascetic view of reality has even less to do with the announcement of the good
news. Jesus was criticized for eating and drinking and for con-
sorting with sinners. His disciples were reproached for breaking
the Sabbath by plucking ears of corn when they were hungry.

Jesus went to dinner parties and weddings.

Jesus did not retreat from society in order to remain pure, as did the Essenes. He did not avoid getting his hands dirty, both figuratively and literally. Jesus' "going apart" for a while, his days of retreat, his moments of solitude are always presented in relationship to his life's work and his involvement with the community. He prayed forty days in the desert before beginning his public ministry (Mk 1:12), again before choosing the Twelve (Mk 3:13); he was praying when the disciples asked him to teach them how to pray (Lk 11); he followed the Jewish custom of celebrating the Passover meal, combining community and prayer, and he prayed in the garden where he was arrested (Lk 22:39). His prayer was intimately connected to his life and his work. The rhythm, the flow between prayer and ministry nourished both, enriched both.

Incarnational asceticism suggests that Jesus suffered and died because of the way he lived. He suffered and died because of what he taught. He suffered and died because of his commitment to alleviate suffering and pain wherever he could. When we realize that the passion and death of Jesus were the result of the teaching and life of Jesus, we are forced to deny credence to any theology that speaks of a God who demanded suffering or who even simply tolerated it.

### It Is Relational

Individual awareness is not the essence of feminist spirituality. Because we are sexual beings, we are capable of relationships, of communication, of community, of communion. Sexuality has to do with our desire for communion, union with another. Our capacity for relationships is dependent on the development of our sexuality. Although each of us experiences human wholeness and uniqueness, although each of us is an individual, not able to be divided, we yearn and long to transcend our separateness. Without human companionship we are incomplete. The gift of sexuality is the source of that longing, the catalyst that makes relationships possible. We love because we are embodied, we love because we are enfleshed, we love because we are incarnate.

Bodiliness, incarnated spirit, is the characteristic of all human beings that makes it possible for us to relate to one another and to God. To be spiritual means that we do not end at our skin; our very being extends to, touches, and is touched by others, becomes so much a part of what is beyond ourselves as to create new realities. Each new relationship generates new life, even as the Spirit is generated from the relationship between the Father and the Son.

Being spiritual is a way of being human. Becoming human depends upon immersion in a community, relating with others; we do not become human in isolation. Spirituality requires not that we divorce ourselves from creation, but that we relate to it in a way that bespeaks our reverence for all that God has created. Spirituality has to do with what we believe, what we hope for, what we love, what we communicate to one another in word and in action.

Women the world over are coming to realize that they can be and often have been unjust when it comes to themselves. In order to truly relate to anyone else, to establish an "I-Thou" relationship, rather than an "I-It" one, a person has to develop an "I." The call to develop one's personhood is not a call to selfish preoccupation. Unless a man or a woman develops into a mature, independent adult, it is impossible to enter into any relationship of mutuality.

Some women have become almost non-persons, defining themselves through husbands or children. They have lived vicariously through them and often in the process thwarted their own spiritual development and that of their families. In discussing Doris Lessing's *Martha Quest*, Judith Plaskow contends that in not taking a test she could easily have passed, Martha is guilty of injustice towards herself.

Instead of attempting to actualize as many of her potentialities as possible, she simply yields to the easiest and closest alternatives before her. Confronted with a familiar path which she does not wish to follow and a more difficult one which she does, she "chooses" the former. Thus, like Paul, she experiences a conflict between her real self and a strange law which controls her. She is self-estranged or in a state of sin.[7]

*Relating to Non-Human Creation*   Christians are caught in a dilemma described by Rosemary Radford Ruether: "On the one hand, humans are said to be guilty for the inadequacies of the rest of creation.... On the other hand, humans bear no responsibility for the rest of creation."[8] All of creation is marred by human sin, yet humans are set over animal and plant life that may be treated as existing only for the good and pleasure of humanity. The modern ecological movement has focused our attention on the relationship between human beings and the rest of creation. We have become more aware that:

> The material substances of our bodies live on in plants and animals, just as our own bodies are composed from minute to minute of substances that once were parts of other animals and plants, stretching back through time to prehistoric ferns and reptiles, to ancient biota that floated in the primal seas of earth.... [Our kinship with all Earth creatures] spans the ages, linking our material substance with all the beings that have gone before us on Earth and even to the dust of the exploding stars.[9]

It may be that because women have been so identified with nature, they are more in tune with its rhythm and are therefore in sympathy with the abuse of nature. The rape of Earth, cruelty to animals, the misuse and exploitation of natural resources are all manifestations of a society that defines most of creation as objects that exist only for the benefit of human beings. The language of "mastering Earth, lording it over it, subduing it..." fosters a mindset that assumes the rightness of hierarchical relationships. The interpretation of the Genesis story that sets humans over the rest of creation, whose only purpose is for human enjoyment and benefit, is being questioned; alternative interpretations are being developed, many of them in the light of feminist thought. Perhaps because we speak of nature as "she," even call it by the name "Mother Nature," women have an affinity for the rest of creation.[10] Whatever the reason, many women appear to have an acute sense of empathy for all of creation.

We might even say that concern for creation is part of a sacramental view of reality. Sacramentality celebrates the ability of things of this world to make God present, or at least to make us aware of that presence. As sacramental people, we believe that palms and oil, ashes and water are holy. We believe that common bread and wine are the sacred presence of Christ in our midst. It is a short step between seeing some branches, some oil and water, some dirt as holy, some bread and wine as sacred, to seeing all trees and water, all soil as signs of the divine involvement in our world. Because some bread is sacred, all bread is sacred.

*Relating to God*      Because we are incarnate, we relate to God incarnately. Relationship with God is not ethereal or other-worldly; it is not intellectual or intangible. Relationship with God does not depend on an antiseptic purity or a denial of the body. Feminists are among those who are searching for a theology of sexuality that is consistent with the Christian message and with their own experience.

> A new way, a new theory or theology of sexual love, will mean starting with accepting yourself as somebody loved by God, a God who accepts you totally, including your body and its sexual drives for oneness and communion. She accepts you when you experience your selfishness and the sexual fantasies that arise from being human, whether you be hetero/homo/bisexual, whether male or female, whether prayerful or confused or lost or not concerned with keeping in touch with God about sex right now. That theology of God's unconditioned love applies to the total you—bodiliness and sexuality included! No wonder the Christian story of God is called the Good News.[11]

As a woman or man embraces feminism (or is embraced by it), the symbols and myths that support patriarchal religion no longer nourish, no longer sustain. The reclaiming of symbols and myths is a long, slow process. And during that time, feminists live with a hunger and a longing for Christian symbols, metaphors, myths, and rituals that will sustain them in their journey. The need to develop a spirituality that reclaims and redefines these symbols and myths may be the most painful part of the conversion to feminism.

The proliferation of women's prayer groups, the sharing and publishing of feminist rituals and liturgies, the number of women who are spiritual directors and retreat leaders for both women and men are all indications of the struggle to develop a way for feminism and Christianity to challenge and to embrace one another.

### It Is Prophetic

A third facet of feminist spirituality is that it is prophetic. The role of the prophet is often a lonely and difficult one. The prophet sees what others may not, sees reality from another perspective, sees connections others miss, sees what is easier to ignore. The prophet in biblical times was not a seer or a fortune teller who could predict the future. The prophet was the person sent by God to recall Israel back to the worship of the one true God when Israel became unjust or oppressive of peoples. The connection was always between the life of the community and God. Injustice, deceit, selfishness, violations of the commandments were denounced not in sociological terms but in theological terms. Human life in all its facets interfaces with divine life. The prophet was the one who would not let Israel forget that.

Feminism as a prophetic movement calls society to transform structures, customs, and behaviors that oppress women. Christian feminism makes the connection between that oppression and the God whom we celebrate as love. Christian feminism is concerned with women as individuals and as a group but it does not end there. It is also concerned with the transformation of society in the light of the gospel message. Christian feminists are searching for ways in which feminist principles may give fresh insights into the gospel, and conversely, for ways in which the gospel may give fresh insights to feminism.

Prophecy is rooted in hope, hope in the lavish goodness of God and in humanity's response to that gift. Hope has little to do with naivete. It ranks among the strong virtues of faith and charity. Augustine links anger and courage with the theological virtue of hope. "Hope has two lovely daughters," he says, "anger, so that what should not be will not be and courage so that what should be will be." We have already discussed the virtue/vice of anger. Let us now turn our attention to courage.

*Courage*     Felicitas, Perpetua, Agatha, Lucy, Agnes, Cecelia, and Anastasia—the women martyrs mentioned in the Canon of the Mass—are only the first in a long line of courageous Christian women. When we speak of courage, Joan of Arc, of course, comes to mind. But many courageous women have been remembered for other qualities and only incidentally for their courage. For example, the creativity and learning of women like Hildegarde of Bingen ought not blind us to her courage. Author, playwright, composer, healer, and abbess, Hildegarde compared herself to the apocryphal Judith as she challenged some of the most powerful leaders of her day.

A story is told that when Hildegarde was in her eighties, she allowed a young man who had been excommunicated to be buried in the convent cemetery. When she refused to follow the bishop's order to remove the body, and even rubbed out the telltale lines around the grave with her cane, the convent was put under interdict. For a year, the church bells were silent, the organ left quiet. More importantly, Mass was not celebrated, sacraments were not given to the sisters. Some called her stubborn, I would call her courageous.

In our own day, can anything compare to the courage of the Mothers of the Plaza del Mayo in Argentina, those women who marched carrying pictures of their disappeared children, risking death themselves. One of them explained their courage thus: "When they take away a child from a woman, they also take away her fear. I have found that the most beautiful way to die is to die for a cause."[12]

Rosa Parks is sometimes remembered as a tired woman who refused to move to the back of the bus. There is more to the story than that. Rosa Parks had learned the basics of civil disobedience, and with full knowledge of the consequences, she defied an unjust law. She was not tired, she was courageous.

We could multiply examples of courageous women, but the

lesson would be the same. Hope, and trust in the promise of the coming reign of God, may be nourished and grow when prophetic anger and courage move us to assume responsibility for bringing about that promised time.

### Feminist Spirituality Empowers

When feminists speak of empowerment they are not referring to a process whereby a woman is "empowered " from without, given power through the agency of another. Empowerment is the process whereby a woman recognizes herself as a mature adult with responsibilities to herself and to the rest of society. Empowerment is a process through which a woman acknowledges and appreciates herself as a person with the gifts necessary to assume that responsibility. It is a process of discovering the breath of God, the spark of divinity within oneself.

One of the common put-downs of feminists is that they just want to get power, they are power hungry. And as a matter of fact, women *are* power hungry, they have been and still are starved of power. This put-down is possible because power has negative overtones in spite of the fact that we speak of an all-powerful God, and scripture repeatedly refers to the power of the Spirit.

Power has been confused with an abuse of power. Manipulation and exploitation are misuses of power, not expressions of it. Feminists are reclaiming the word power and the right to exercise power in their own lives and relationships. Power is not a closed entity with just so much of it available so that "giving over power" diminishes power. Like truth, beauty, and wisdom, it is not diminished in the sharing. Power in itself is neutral. It is how we handle power that determines its value.

Power does not exist in a vacuum. It is a characteristic of relationships. The nature of the relationship determines in great measure the morality or immorality of the use of power. Power may be over others, against them, for them, or with them. Power that exploits or manipulates others corrupts, but power may also be nutritive—for others; integrative-with others. Power may also be competitive. Competitive power may be destructive, but it may also stretch us to accomplish what appears beyond our grasp.[13]

Power is a significant spiritual issue for feminists since women have been defined for so long as innocent—as in "innocent women and children." Women have been so considered because they were not responsible for the decisions whose consequences destroyed life, they were not responsible for waging war, they were not responsible for instituting programs that destroy the Earth, they were not responsible for history's atrocities. But that is a false guiltlessness; a pseudo-innocence. Such powerlessness is not worthy of the name virtue because it derives from a lack of mature responsibility. If we doubt that powerlessness is not a virtue, we have only to think of how our society scorns powerless men. Such innocence is ridiculed in a man.

As a liberative praxis, feminism has to do with radically changing the patriarchal understandings of power, which are operative even in the feminist movement. Anglo feminists need to remember that in order to undo patriarchy, we must create societies in which people can be self-defining and self-determining. To achieve this, power has to be transformed and shared.[14]

In addressing some of the so-called strong virtues like anger, courage, and power in this chapter, I do not mean to negate the more nurturing virtues of care, compassion, gentility, purity, and generosity. I have not included these in this discussion for two reasons. Women have been encultured over the ages to develop these characteristics and many women have embraced them to a heroic degree. Secondly, there is no dearth of material already written for women that calls them to the more "feminine" virtues.

### Questions for Reflection

1. What connections do you make between sexuality and spirituality? Have you ever pondered the connection? Does it make sense to you?

2. What do you think God's involvement with human suffering is?

3. How does your relationship with God manifest itself in your relationships with other people? With Earth?

4. How can women develop the so-called strong virtues without losing the more nurturing ones?

5. What is your definition of power? Do you feel empowered to accept responsibility for your own life? Why or why not?

### Endnotes

1. The nineteen- and twenty-year-old men who had been trained to hate and to kill, found themselves carrying out a carnage they did not know themselves capable of. They live with the horror of that knowledge, even as the villagers live with the fear, mistrust, and hatred of men who only days before had brought chocolates.

2. *Encyclopedia Judaica* 13 (New York: Macmillan, 1971) 1405.

3. Robert McAfee Brown, *Spirituality and Liberation: Overcoming the Great Fallacy* (Philadelphia: Westminster, 1988) 74.

4. Joanne Carlson Brown and Rebecca Parker, "For God So Loved the World" in *Christianity, Patriarchy and Abuse: A Feminist Critique* edited by Joanne Carlson Brown and Carole R. Bohn (New York: Pilgrim Press, 1989) 23.

5. Elie Wiesel, *The Trial of God (As It Was Held on February 25, 1649, in Shamgord)* (New York: Random House, 1979).

6. Brown and Parker, "For God So Loved the World," 27.

7. Judith Plaskow, *Sex, Sin and Grace* (Washington: University of America Press, 1980) 115.

8. Rosemary Radford Ruether, *Gaia and God: An Ecofeminist Theology of Earth Healing* (San Francisco: HarperCollins, 1992).

9. Ibid., 252.

10. Ibid., 195. Ruether calls our attention to the work of Robert Bacon, the father of the scientific method. He speaks of nature as female "to be coerced, penetrated, conquered, forced to yield, the language of the rape and subjugation of women."

11. Dody Donnelly, *Radical Love: An Approach to Sexual Spirituality*, 55.

12. Hebe Bonafini, from a report in *La Voz Semanal*, June 16, 1985. Quoted in *Through Her Eyes: Women's Theology from Latin America* edited by Elsa Tamez (Maryknoll: Orbis Books, 1989) 85.

13. *Power and Innocence.*

14. Isasi-Diaz, *Inheriting Our Mother's Garden*, 96-97.

# Conclusion

There is a chapter yet to be written before this book is complete. But it is not one that I am able to write. It concerns what each of us will do with the wisdom and the knowledge that women like Hagar and Magdalen, Vashti and Lilith, Teresa of Avila and Simone Weil, Dorothy Day and Theresa Kane have willed to us. It is about our response to the contributions of women like Rosemary Radford Ruether, Elisabeth Schüssler Fiorenza, Letty Russell, Catherine LaCugna, and Elizabeth Johnson. The chapter is about taking seriously what it means to receive the gifts that these women have bestowed.

Books are not meant to be swallowed whole, digested only to be regurgitated. To really read a book is to rewrite it. To enter into conversation with a book is to advance the conversation, challenge some ideas, affirm others, create new knowledge. To really read a book is to put our own experience, thoughts, ideas, and values into the conversation.

This book, like others, is not merely for the acquisition of new information or deeper insights about women and Christianity. In searching for religiously significant data, we draw on our tradition, on the wisdom and insights of our time, and on our own experience. All three are partners in the conversation. I have attempted to place the wisdom of the Christian tradition in dialogue with the wisdom of women in our time. My hope is that this dialogue will challenge each reader to enter into the conversation, bring her or his own experience to it, and then compose a concluding chapter.

That concluding chapter will then not just be words on paper. Rather, it will be a commitment to the values of Christian feminism because feminist liberation theology is not merely an intellectual exercise. Like other liberation theologies, it demands both the transformation of individual lives and commitment to the transformation of the world.

# $\mathcal{B}$ibliography

Belenky, Mary Field, et al. *Women's Ways of Knowing: The Development of Self, Voice and Mind*. New York: Basic Books, 1986.

Brown, Joanne Carlson, and Carole R. Bohn, eds. *Christianity, Patriarchy and Abuse*. New York: Pilgrim Press, 1989.

Carr, Anne E. *Transforming Grace*. San Francisco: Harper & Row, 1988.

Chittister, Joan. *Winds of Change: Women Challenge Church*. Kansas City: Sheed & Ward, 1986.

Conn, Joan Wolski, ed. *Women's Spirituality: Resources for Christian Development*. New York: Paulist Press, 1986.

Daly, Mary. *Beyond God the Father: Toward a Philosophy of Women's Liberation*. Boston: Beacon Press, 1973.

Daly, Mary. *Gyn-Ecology: The Metaethics of Radical Feminism*. Boston: Beacon Press, 1978.

Fabella, Virginia. *We Dare to Dream: Doing Theology as Asian Women*. Hong Kong: Asian Women's Resource Center for Culture and Theology, 1989.

Fabella, Virginia, Mercy Amba Oduyoye. *With Passion and Compassion: Third World Women Doing Theology*. Maryknoll, N.Y.: Orbis Books, 1988.

Fiorenza, Elisabeth Schüssler, and Mary Collins, eds. *Women: Invisible in the Church and Theology.* (Concilium) Edinburgh: T. & T. Clark, 1985.

Fiorenza, Elisabeth Schüssler. *Bread Not Stone.* Boston: Beacon Press, 1984.

Fiorenza, Elisabeth Schüssler. *But She Said: Feminist Practices of Biblical Interpretation.* Boston: Beacon Press, 1992.

Fiorenza, Elisabeth Schüssler. *In Memory of Her: A Feminist Theological Reconstruction of Christian Origins.* New York: Crossroad, 1983.

Gebara, Ivone, and Maria C. Bingemer. *Mary: Mother of God, Mother of the Poor.* Maryknoll, N.Y.: Orbis Books, 1989.

Gilligan, Carol. *In a Different Voice.* Cambridge, Mass.: Harvard University Press, 1982.

Grant, Jacqueline. *White Women's Christ and Black Women's Jesus.* Atlanta: Scholars Press, 1989.

Harris, Maria. *Dance of the Spirit: The Seven Steps of Women's Spirituality.* New York: Bantam, 1989.

Isasi-Diaz, Ada, and Yolanda Tarango. *Hispanic Women.* San Francisco: Harper & Row, 1988.

Johnson, Elizabeth. *Consider Jesus: Waves of Renewal in Christology.* New York: Crossroad, 1990.

Johnson, Elizabeth. *She Who Is: The Mystery of God in Feminist Theological Discourse.* New York: Crossroad, 1993.

Johnson, Elizabeth. *Women, Earth and the Creator Spirit.* Mahwah, N.J.: Paulist Press, 1993.

Katoppo, Marianne. *Compassionate and Free.* Maryknoll, N.Y.: Orbis Books, 1979.

LaCugna, Catherine. *God With Us: The Trinity and Christian Life.* New York: Crossroad, 1991.

McFague, Sallie. *Metaphorical Theology: Models of God in Religious Language.* Philadelphia: Fortress Pres, 1982.

McFague, Sallie. *Models of God: Theology for an Ecological Nuclear Age.* Philadelphia: Fortress Press, 1987.

Miller, Jean Baker. *Toward a New Psychology of Women* (rev. ed). Boston: Beacon Press, 1991.

O'Connor, Francis Bernard. *Like Bread Their Voices Rise: Global Women Challenge the Church*. Notre Dame, Ave Maria Press, 1993.

Oduyoye, Mercy Amba, and Musimbi B.A. Kanyoro, eds. *The Will to Arise: Women, Tradition and the Church in Africa*. Maryknoll, N.Y.: Orbis Books, 1992.

Osiek, Carolyn, RSCJ. *Beyond Anger: On Being a Feminist in the Church*. New York: Paulist Press, 1986.

Plaskow, Judith. *Standing Again at Sinai: Judaism From a Feminist Perspective*. San Francisco: Harper & Row, 1990.

Proctor-Smith, Marjorie. *In Her Own Rite: Constructing a Feminist Liturgical Tradition*. Nashville: Abingdon, 1990.

Ruether, Rosemary Radford, and Rosemary Skinner Keller, eds. *Women & Religion in America, Vol 1: The Nineteenth Century*. San Francisco: Harper & Row, 1988.

Ruether, Rosemary Radford, and Rosemary Skinner Keller, eds. *Women & Religion in America, Vol 2: The Colonial and Revolutionary Periods*. San Francisco: Harper & Row, 1988.

Ruether, Rosemary Radford, and Rosemary Skinner Keller, eds. *Women & Religion in America, Vol 3: The Twentieth Century*. San Francisco: Harper & Row, 1986.

Ruether, Rosemary Radford. *Gaia and God: An Eco-Feminist Theology of Earth Healing*. New York: HarperCollins, 1992.

Ruether, Rosemary Radford. *Sexism and God-Talk: Toward a Feminist Theology*. Boston: Beacon Press, 1983.

Russell, Letty M., et al., eds. *Inheriting Our Mothers' Gardens: Feminist Theology in Third World Perspective*. Philadelphia: Westminster Press, 1988.

Schneiders, Sandra. *Women and the Word: The Gender of God in the New Testament and the Spirituality of Women*. New York: Paulist Press, 1986.

Stuhlmueller, Carroll, ed. *Women and Priesthood*. Collegeville, Minn.: The Liturgical Press, 1978.

Swidler, Leonard, Arlene Swidler. *Women Priests: A Catholic Commentary on the Vatican Declaration*. New York: Paulist Press, 1977.

Tamez, Elsa. *Through Her Eyes: Women's Theology in Latin America*. Maryknoll, N.Y.: Orbis Books, 1988.

Trible, Phyllis. *God and the Rhetoric of Sexuality*. Philadelphia: Fortress Press, 1978.

Trible, Phyllis. *Texts of Terror*. Philadelphia: Fortress Press, 1984.

Warner, Marina. *Alone of All Her Sex*. New York: Alfred A. Knopf, 1976.

Weaver, Mary Jo. *New Catholic Women: A Contemporary Challenge to Traditional Religious Authority*. San Francisco: Harper & Row, 1985.

Weems, Renita J. *Just a Sister Away: A Womanist Vision of Women's Relationships in the Bible*. San Diego: LuraMedia, 1988.

Wilson-Kastner, Patricia. *Faith, Feminism, and the Church*. Philadelphia: Fortress Press, 1983.

# Index of Subjects

# Of Related Interest...

## The Hope for Wholeness
*A Spirituality for Feminists*
Katherine Zappone
The author maps out a clear path, one that points to the necessity of finding a wholeness that all—women and men alike—can embrace. She concludes that investigating the various feminist spiritualities will transform this wholeness from a hope to a reality.

ISBN: 0-89622-495-3, 195 pp, $12.95

## Feminism, Redemption and the Christian Tradition
Mary Grey
Based on the belief that within Christian tradition there is a liberating dream to be recovered, this book poses the argument that to reclaim this dream, women must recover a positive sense of self that can ultimately lead to a new experience of redemption.

ISBN: 0-89622-428-7, 250 pp, $16.95

## The Christology of Rosemary Radford Ruether
*A Critical Introduction*
Mary Hembrow Snyder
Readers are introduced to the forceful ideas, widespread community and political involvement, and far-reaching religious theory of Ruether. The book explores the implications of Ruether's theology for ecumenism, spirituality, soteriology, theological method and the church's self-understanding.

ISBN: 0-89622-358-2, 152 pp, $12.95

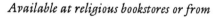

*Available at religious bookstores or from*

TWENTY-THIRD PUBLICATIONS
P.O. Box 180 • Mystic, CT 06355
1-800-321-0411